I0033510

The Intentional Mindset

The Intentional Mindset

Data, Decisions, and Your Destiny

Jane Frankel

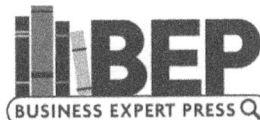

BEP

BUSINESS EXPERT PRESS

Leader in applied, concise business books

The Intentional Mindset: Data, Decisions, and Your Destiny

Copyright © Business Expert Press, LLC, 2023.

Cover design by Charlene Kronstedt

Interior design by Exeter Premedia Services Private Ltd., Chennai, India

All rights reserved. No part of this publication may be reproduced, stored in a retrieval system, or transmitted in any form or by any means—electronic, mechanical, photocopy, recording, or any other except for brief quotations, not to exceed 400 words, without the prior permission of the publisher.

First published in 2023 by
Business Expert Press, LLC
222 East 46th Street, New York, NY 10017
www.businessexpertpress.com

ISBN-13: 978-1-63742-489-6 (paperback)
ISBN-13: 978-1-63742-490-2 (e-book)

Business Expert Press Business Career Development Collection

First edition: 2023

10 9 8 7 6 5 4 3 2 1

Description

Do you *derail* yourself or do you *propel* yourself toward success? Your decisions lead to your destiny. You can make good decisions or bad decisions. These decisions are very often based on your mindset. Recognizing the power of your mindset is essential to reaching your destiny. Your mindset includes your goals, values, beliefs, and mode of work. It provides the framework for how you think, how you behave, and why you make decisions. Understanding your mindset puts you in control of your life.

The 21st century world of work requires workers to make good and relevant decisions. This book contains thought-provoking insights into your decisions that drive your success. It speaks to anyone who would like to create and navigate a personal environment for individual success toward a desired destiny.

Keywords

mindset of awareness; intentional mindset; controlling mindset; beliefs and biases; narrative; inquiry; lifelong learning; autonomous work; autonomy and learning; mode of work; stakeholders; a knowledge mindset; origins of mindset; knowledge environments; functions of mindset; goals; values; beliefs; biases

Contents

Testimonials

"This book stimulated my curiosity, animated my desire to succeed, and made me want to read on."—**Donald Wargo, Associate Professor of Economics, Temple University, Philadelphia, PA**

"In my experience, The Intentional Mindset's *greatest asset comes from its interpersonal implications. Particularly, this book's contents and workshop materials inspire conversation between both students and colleagues, ultimately deepening readers' understanding of their position both in work and in life. In short, as much as I enjoyed learning about the application of my own values and beliefs in my life, I also benefitted greatly from hearing about and interacting with others' experiences doing the same."*—**Ryan Zajdel, Economics Graduate, 2023 Temple University, Philadelphia, PA**

"We found it very interesting and a great way to help individuals and organizations to focus on productively (efficiently and effectively) achieving their goals short term as well as providing a process for achieving goals throughout their lifetimes."—**Terry Hartman, Retired Director, Vera Jackson Scholarship, and Bill Hartman, Retired Partner, Ernst and Young**

"Loved chapter 1. I will share with my recently graduated son to help with his career management."—**Lisa Lemire, Managing Member, Kamini Bay Asset Management, LLC**

"I am sending this book to every one of my children and their spouses."—**Kathy Roth, Administrative Assistant, University of Delaware**

Preface

My career experiences have been very diverse, from teaching K to 12 to creating user education programs for private sector technology companies to defining and developing knowledge work skills for universities and the emerging workforce. A major lesson that I took away from these experiences is that people in all settings do not always make good decisions for themselves. This is partially because we have lived in small groups for so long that thinking evolved to be local, as opposed to global as we need it to be today. They make these compromised decisions based on short-term needs, lack of research into a situation, or lack of awareness of what prompts certain behaviors and decisions. I concluded that if people can understand the rationale behind their own behaviors and decisions, as well as the behaviors and decisions of their colleagues, there is a much better chance of managing that decision making for better outcomes. This is a matter of exploring your mindset, which includes your goals, values, beliefs, and mode of work. Managing these elements of mindset enables more focus for relevant decision making.

Behavioral economists observe that a large percentage of decision making is based on your mindset. It seems a worthy pursuit to explore this mindset and how to use it to your advantage in decision making for your best outcomes and destinies. As I recalled specific experiences, they sparked an analysis of a mindset for insights into how these mindsets work separately and together to guide good decision making. Each chapter in this book is focused on one of these experiences.

Your biggest challenge today is how the world of work has changed in the knowledge economy. Work conditions are challenging in new ways due to acceleration of technology, climate change, and globalization. Additional challenges today include political extremism, economic barriers, pandemics, and social tensions. But challenges also provide more opportunity to find new options for success. Managing your mindset to master and take advantage of these challenges through expert decision making is not only possible, but also essential if you are to survive and thrive in this economy. A clearer understanding of those challenges and how to manage them through your own power of mindset is presented here. You have the ability to take better care of yourself if you strive to use your mindset to be autonomous, introspective, and collaborative in your activities. Awareness of mindset, inquiry, and learning will help you make good decisions for sustainability and growth for yourself and/or your organization. I aim to share some ideas on how to explore, understand, and manage your mindset for decisions that lead to desired outcomes.

I am hoping you will choose to develop an enabling awareness of your mindset and those of others in order to ensure the destiny that you seek.

Acknowledgments

Many people have helped with this book and I am appreciative for all of them and their interest in this project.

Ben Frankel, my husband and Education Professor, provided unending research support. Bill Hartman, a corporate consulting executive, gave early and final reviews on topic feasibility, content, and flow for defined audiences. Terry Hartman, Board Member of Vera Jackson Scholarship Foundation, reviewed for relevant emerging workforce guidance. Donald Wargo, a Behavioral Economics Professor, provided significant insights into behavioral tendencies and referrals to expert research. Suzanne Garber, a corporate health care executive, contributed general review of content presentation. Lisa Lemire, a financial investment executive, reviewed for sequencing of topics and content flow. Dylan Baird of Philly Foodworks and Russ Starke of Think Company provided case study stories and review.

Thank you, All.

Introduction

The Intentional Mindset

A large group of senior executives sought to guide more junior members of the business community in their skills and development toward success. They engaged in a mentor program focused on regional universities and small businesses that needed help with training young workforce candidates. The mentors defined the program with mindset awareness and control, project structures, and implementation work needed to achieve success. This intentional thinking structure supported the mentors and mentees as each had a goal for the work to be achieved. Mentors wanted to influence and enable mindsets for positive work, as well as learn about their mentee's specific and individual needs. Mentees wanted to acquire skills to reach their work goals to contribute to their individual growth plans. The program was about ten weeks long, giving the mentors and mentees time to get acquainted, build trust and relationship, and ultimately develop some 21st century knowledge work skills and mindsets for autonomous goal achievement. The program was deemed a success as everyone learned from the experience and all met their goals.

You work to achieve some success. The way you think about your work, and, subsequently, your work will meet success or not. Is your goal the right one? Do you value the goal and work for relevant reasons? Will you derail yourself and your success or will you propel yourself toward that success? Your decisions lead to your destiny and your legacy. You can make optimal decisions or poor decisions. And very often these decisions are based on your mindset. Recognizing and using the power of your mindset is essential to defining and reaching success. What does that mindset include? It includes your goals, values, beliefs, and mode of work. It provides the framework for how you think, how you behave, and why you make certain decisions as opposed to others. Exploring these mindset components leads to a full understanding of why you decide what you decide and, perhaps, how to change your mindset to serve you better in your decision making. Further, these mindset components must be compatible with each other, as well as to those of your stakeholders for reaching success. This will create a common mindset to guide all work.

Mindsets are just facts of life. Everyone has goals, values, beliefs, and modes of work. As these mindsets guide decision making, awareness of them is essential to their management and alignment for best decision-making results. The 21st century work is collaborative, so mindset awareness is essential to increase the ability to work together. Matching mindset components with others is the challenge, not allowing yourself to be distracted with judging the good or bad aspects of another's thinking. It is rather a task in understanding so that you can manage, adapt, and/or reinforce diverse mindsets to achieve the outcomes you desire. Exploring mindsets cannot be avoided if you want to be in control of your destiny.

> **Do you know how and what drives your decisions?**

Data, Information, and Knowledge

The information age of late, providing volumes of data and information, has evolved into the knowledge economy of the 21st century. The evolution happens when data and information are converted to the knowledge that guides all of your work. Knowledge workers, those who make this conversion, are continuous decision makers. Your mindset provides the frame for making those decisions, as it determines what data and information you consider when building knowledge. If you value money and your goal is to be a millionaire before age 25, you may not be interested in data about the value of building a strong community or aligning to stakeholders and their needs. You instead would be researching financial models that double and triple investment in a short period of time. You would miss out on considering data regarding community programs to enhance the quality of life for its members, which, in turn, could create a market of another type to generate revenue.

Acceleration

Knowledge economy conditions also include the acceleration of technology, environment/energy issues, and globalization (Friedman 2016) to be navigated. These accelerations further create the need for autonomous thinking and work. In an accelerated world, decisions are made with lightning speed. Autonomous individuals and organizations are much more productive because everyone is responsible for thinking and not waiting for one person to make decisions. Fifty thinkers who are aligned with a common mindset are certainly more impactful than one who thinks for everyone. So the common mindset becomes essential to expedite decisions.

Decision makers must work autonomously as they consider data and information to create knowledge, which allows solid decisions. This autonomy includes both independent and dependent work. The independence of autonomy gives you control of your work and the dependence seeks other's expertise to complement your own expertise. Knowledge workers make decisions but only after inquiry and learning have brought insight to the decision. Building autonomous mindsets that enable inquiry and learning for decision making, for yourself and with your stakeholders, is essential in the knowledge economy. It is essential that knowledge workers have mindsets that value inquiry and learning, allowing them to continuously evaluate their own thinking and that of their stakeholders to ensure clarity and overarching alignment for successful decisions.

Understanding and using mindset propels a project to success, your own or that of an organization. A community mindset can minimize challenges within project, customer, partner, and/or merged environments. It facilitates and clarifies work with an environment that motivates knowledge workers to inquire, learn, and build knowledge to guide decisions. This community mindset leads knowledge workers to highest performance. Figure I.1 represents the structure of a mindset.

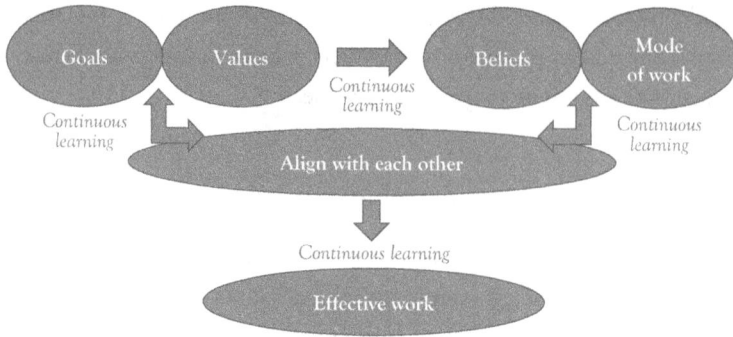

Figure I.1 A mindset: self and stakeholders

Knowledge Worker Mindset

Autonomy and learning go together to create the knowledge worker mindset. The first priority of learning is to understand your own mindset and how it impacts decisions toward your success. Does your goal match your values and your beliefs, as demonstrated by your mode of work? If they are not aligned, you will work against yourself and fail to meet expected results. Then you can turn to evaluating your stakeholders' mindsets for alignment, as well. Managers and workers both need awareness and control of their mindsets. Managers set the environment that enables workers to maximize their mindsets for highest productivity and performance, individually and as an organization.

Philosophers describe how mindsets impact society and the actions people take that preserve or change society. Conversely, this same society impacts individuals for good or for bad. It makes sense to understand this connection as best as you can through an understanding of mindset components, what created yours, and how you need to manage them. Ultimately, does your mindset need alternation to lead to better outcomes?

Philly Foodworks is a farm to table initiative that provides fresh vegetables from regional farms to local neighborhoods and families. The business model, although sound, needed to grow in order to sustain its value to its founder and the families that benefit from the company's service. Dylan Baird, the founder, had to create an organizational infrastructure for his employees that would facilitate the collaborative effort to acquire like-minded businesses to expand his reach to customers and Philly Foodworks' volume of vegetables. His team had to embrace and sort out the goals and values of each organization with which they would work, as well as make individual decisions on critical path actions to support company growth. The team identified the acquired businesses' mindsets and needs as they considered them stakeholders for each partnership or acquisition they engaged.

Additionally, Philly Foodworks' business increased by 400 percent in two months due to the pandemic of 2020 and advances in technology. Baird was challenged with evolving the organization to manage this growth with his small staff. He hired about 40 new staffers and entrusted decision making to all staff members from a common mindset platform. The platform included expectations of autonomous inquiry, research, learning, peer decision review, and first-hand knowledge of customer needs. This approach allowed the company to grow, survive, and thrive in very challenging times.

Summary: Seeking a New Intentional Mindset

To quote Lord Buddha (Bodhipaksa 2014), "Mental states are preceded by mind, have mind as their master, are created by mind." This statement describes the catalyst for designing and building your mindsets to serve you well.

If you are aware of and monitor your thinking, you can be an expert learner, positioned to thrive. My goal is to help you, the reader, become aware of how you think currently, how that mindset drives your behaviors and decisions, the impact that those decisions are having on your outcomes, and how you can manage your mindset to support and/or alter your thinking for your desired destiny. Hopefully, you will recognize that the effort necessary to build a conscious or intentional mindset to achieve this is worthwhile as you define and achieve the destiny that you desire.

Learning (Waitzkin 2007) happens "by studying discrete pieces of information thoroughly and practicing their application repetitively,… they eventually shed their technical, nitty-gritty character…shifts… from the conscious mind to the unconscious mind where it can connect with other chunks of internalized knowledge and manifest as the sudden burst of insight we experience as free-flowing intuition."

Waitzkin used this learning concentration to become a champion chess player and, then, a champion in martial arts.

Thinking happens according to a platform of goals, values, beliefs, and modes of work, which makes up a mindset. Responses to daily situations are often unconscious as directed by that mindset. Through awareness you can migrate to a more intentional thinking model. Ideally, you can eventually make that new, more conscious and intentional thinking model into a new unconscious model for automatic and productive thinking, behaviors, and decisions.

Four Sections of the Book

The Intentional Mindset: Data, Decision, and Your Destiny describes the components of mindset, the impact of mindset, how to shape it, and how leaders and managers can manage it within their organizations for best results. It includes four sections: *Understanding Mindset, Building an Autonomous Mindset, Using a Learning System, and Building an Environment to Support Autonomous Work.* Each section includes relevant discussions to guide your development of an autonomous mindset to maximize your ability to meet your destiny with no exceptions.

Each chapter includes thought-provoking questions integrated into the content to help you internalize the concepts presented. There is also a Call to Action at the end of Chapters 5 through 9, where you can apply ideas to your own world and work. I suggest using a journal to record your thoughts and answers as you come across these questions and Calls to Action. You may also find that you will want to go back and rethink some of those answers as you continue reading. Thinking and reflecting on that thinking is an important tenet of the learning mindset, which we all strive for in the knowledge economy.

Contributing Disciplines

Multiple disciplines of study have been referenced to guide the ideas presented in this book. Topics and references on anthropology, psychology, sociology, strategic management, behavioral economics, economics, intrapreneurship, and entrepreneurship are combined to support these ideas and calls to action.

Disclaimer 1: My research and experiences led me to define the mindset system as I see it and have presented it here. There are undoubtedly many more interpretations and dimensions to the topic of mindset. I only offer this one as it hopefully will be useful in an applied manner to anyone who wishes to ensure autonomy and success in knowledge economy endeavors.

Disclaimer 2: The stories presented are real but the names of the participants have been changed in some cases.

Disclaimer 3: You will find some redundancy on the basic concepts of mindset, autonomy, stakeholders, and narrative in various chapters. This is intentional for the purpose of reinforcing these important concepts and to allow readers to use chapters individually and not be dependent on the content of a previous chapter.

SECTION I
Understanding Mindset

CHAPTER 1

The Knowledge Economy

The 21st century introduces major challenges in the workplace that require an awareness of mindset, how and what you think, and how that thinking leads to decision

> **The 21st century knowledge economy demands new skills and insights.**

making. These challenges include globalization, acceleration of technology, and environmental issues (Friedman 2016). World leaders at a 21st century World Economic Forum challenged workers to find new ways to create value from the vast amounts of data and information that were collected in the recent information age. Data and information availability is a major achievement in the history of data science, but now it must be applied to work to create knowledge that can lead to new value. Thus, the 21st century has become known as a knowledge economy, engaging knowledge workers to systematically create that new value. Technology acceleration is a positive force for creating knowledge from data and information as it automates data and information availability and management. But globalization and the environment impose new complexities on work in the 21st century, introducing new issues to be solved. The acceleration of all three areas requires knowledge workers to be autonomous learners who continuously make decisions. These requirements dictate how you work. Figure 1.1 models the current state and management of these 21st century accelerations and complexity.

Work in the 21st century is fast, often remote, continuously changing, technology-driven, and involves working with stakeholders who you most likely do not know. It is the requirement for autonomous work and decision making that makes your mindset so important. This mindset, including your goals, values, beliefs, and mode of work, controls how you think, what you think, and, therefore, what you decide.

Technology enables climate and globalization in managing challenges of change, autonomy, and connectivity.

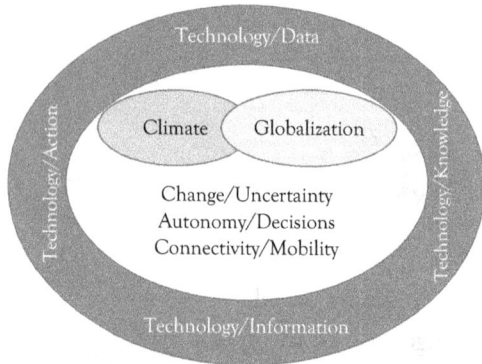

Technology/Data

Climate   Globalization

Change/Uncertainty
Autonomy/Decisions
Connectivity/Mobility

Technology/Action

Technology/Knowledge

Technology/Information

Figure 1.1 Complexity in our 21st century world

Mindset components define what, when, and how you learn—the basis of your autonomous decisions. Your decisions control your destiny and legacy. Your mindset and thinking cannot be left to chance. Exploring your mindset and how it impacts your thinking and decisions is urgent, important, and feasible.

The key ideas in this chapter include:

- Knowledge as the newest resource
- New work needs: autonomous thinking guided by mindset
- Fulfilling those needs: managing oneself
- Sample changes to the economy
- The seven skills of autonomy
- An autonomous environment to support autonomous skills

Knowledge as the Newest Resource

Historically, economic resources were categorized into land, labor, and capital. The knowledge economy adds a fourth resource, knowledge. It has overtaken the other resources in importance as it guides the use of the other resources. Since knowledge directs the best and most productive use of each of these other resources, it is essential that 21st century workers have the ability to convert data and information into knowledge to direct action plans for an efficient use of other resources. These workers are called knowledge workers.

Knowledge economy accelerations have made it challenging to consider all of the contributing factors to a decision. In describing these challenges, Friedman in his book, *Thank You for Being Late,* suggests that people take their time to think and rethink, even if it makes them late in meeting expectations. Thinking yields the best results. He is describing and advocating 21st century autonomy, in which you take control of your work and outcomes through structured learning.

The 2020 worldwide pandemic significantly impacted this already challenging environment, as work had to be remote in order to avoid spreading of the worldwide virus. This new remote work reinforced the need for autonomy through learning. Employers also had to revise their working modes to accommodate these workers on whom they depend to sustain their enterprises. So much change was imposed upon people. Mindset has never been more important in meeting the requirements of these changes.

Challenges are especially difficult when they include other people, known as your stakeholders. These stakeholders are all of those who can impact your work and goals in any way. They often have diverse mindsets, and working together requires a common community mindset for work to be productive and meet the common goal of the work. Mergers and acquisitions, partnerships, global trade, remote work with colleagues, and project delays all require a solid understanding of the people you will work with, how you think about yourself, how you think about them, and how they think about you. What is common and what is not? The first challenge in this work is aligning mindsets to guide joint thinking on decisions in your collaborative work.

For knowledge workers who are autonomous decision makers, knowledge is critical to those decisions. Creating knowledge is based on the importance of learning. This learning is systematized through the knowledge pyramid and Bloom's taxonomy of seven levels of thinking and inquiry (Armstrong 2010). Figure 1.2 shows these thinking and inquiry levels as they guide data, information, and knowledge to create an action plan.

Think about how many things have changed in your life over the last year. All change impacts your existence in some way. Awareness allows you to mitigate and maximize the impact of change. In the 21st century environment, change is not only ever present but happens in such an

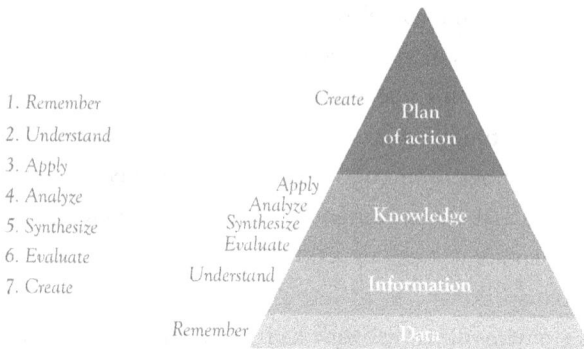

Figure 1.2 **The knowledge pyramid and Bloom's taxonomy**

1. Remember
2. Understand
3. Apply
4. Analyze
5. Synthesize
6. Evaluate
7. Create

accelerated fashion that keeping up with it requires constant attention and learning. The self-sufficiency of autonomy, based on learning and knowledge, gives you control. Without that control, you are subject to whomever or whatever takes control.

New Work Needs: Autonomous Thinking Guided by Mindset

Autonomy, independent and dependent work, depends on your mindset. You act independently based on your goals, values, beliefs, and mode of work. They guide your decisions while working. When trying to sort through a great success or a dismal failure, mindset is the place to start your analysis. Considering the mindset that drove actions, decisions, and outcomes is very insightful for redirecting work and/or tackling the next project. This analysis requires a continuous dependence on learning, which is at the heart of autonomy.

To clarify mindset components, goals set the targets; values set the core principles of your life; beliefs shape your biases, opinions, and assumptions; and mode of work is how you work that reflects the other components. Aligning these components to support each other is of utmost importance. If they do not align, you are working against yourself and will derail your efforts toward your goals. Figure 1.3 describes the connection among the mindset components.

> **Do I have the right goal for the actual work that I am doing?**

Goals tell what.

Values tell why.

Beliefs tell how to manage values.

Mode of work tells how, who, and when.

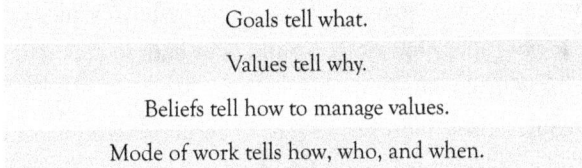

Figure 1.3 Mindset components

Fred, a freshman quarterback for a large university, had been playing football since he was 10 years old. He was good at the game and he loved the team experience. His goal was to play university football. Once he achieved this goal, he compared his longer-term life goals of corporate success to the football experience and the time expectations of his coaches and teammates. They did not match. Fred knew he needed to alter his work and time on the football field to be more supportive of establishing a corporate career. He gave up his quarterback position and pursued membership in three university business associations.

When working within a community, you need an awareness of the community mindset as well as the members' mindsets to guide collaborative actions and decisions toward a common goal and work. Do all members of the community have the same goal for the work that you are doing together? Do members' community values, beliefs, and modes of work support that goal?

When mindsets focus on learning, they enable you to identify your own mindset components and those of others. Inquiry and learning which mindset component drove a decision or why someone else made a seemingly curious choice is the first step in understanding and managing mindset to achieve the results you desire. This book intends to introduce the right questions to help you explore the mindset you hold, the mindset you will need, and the mindsets of others to effectively pursue and achieve your goals.

Reflecting on your experiences holds great insight. Why did you say what you said? Why did you align yourself with a friend's position when you knew he was not being honest? Why did you cancel your appointments to take care of a family member? What was it about a situation that made you try to trick a friend? What mindset component prompted a success when you were prepared for a dismal failure? What do you aim to achieve in your life? How do you build your path to that achievement? What would you like your mindset to have been in order to change a recent outcome? These inquiries all lead to an understanding of how you think, what you think, why you think that, and how that thinking led to an outcome.

Behavioral economists (Ariely 2009; Galef 2021; Vedantam and Mesler 2021) have been curious as to why people don't make economically logical decisions when faced with the many choices and decisions they make every day. These scientists have identified several beliefs that contribute to a mindset and can lead to seemingly illogical decisions, such as:

- Confirmation, the need to confirm what you already believe
- Delusional thinking, managing actions in the context of what you want to be true
- Scout or soldier thinking, assertive or passive responses and actions
- Fear, the intimidation of anticipated results of an action
- Entitlement, the belief that you are owed something
- Risk, the fear of an unpleasant outcome
- Overconfidence, the belief that you will always succeed, no matter what occurs
- Group thinking, actions dictated by members of a group

These behavioral tendencies demonstrate your mindset that impacts your decisions. Knowing about them allows you to manage them for better outcomes.

Fulfilling Those Needs: Managing Oneself

Managing Oneself (Drucker 2005) discusses the need to manage yourself by being responsible and accountable to yourself, the art of self-determinism. Drucker observes that a person has three dimensions to manage: strengths, values, and mode of work. This thinking suggests the importance of an autonomous mindset.

Baird, founder of Philly Foodworks, understood his strengths, values, and mode of work and maximized them to sustain himself and his company. He made changes in his early career because he was not comfortable with the direction of his employer. His strengths and values were not being used so he created a new mode of work for himself with the founding of his own company. He also used these characteristics to define his new venture and its operations that created an autonomous environment for success. All employees were empowered for decision making and responsible for the learning needed to support those decisions.

Autonomy is a complex concept since it integrates independence in taking control with dependence on other's expertise. No one has all the data, information, or answers to the complex challenges and situations that present themselves in the 21st century. These challenges require that 21st century knowledge workers establish autonomous independence and dependence in order to work to accommodate them.

Drucker's concept of self-determinism builds the autonomy needed for surviving and thriving in the knowledge economy. Self-determinism and autonomy define a mindset that values learning about yourself and your stakeholders, which builds a community mindset to align work for success toward a common goal.

Derek Jeter, 2021 Baseball Hall of Famer, led the Yankees in singles, making him a team player. He was praised on his selfless playing as opposed to seeking home run statistics for his own record. His goal was to win the game by supporting team members' achievements. A single can lead to more runs, while a home run is only one run scored. His expertise and contributions considered his dependence on others to get to a win, as well as the independence of his own efforts. In his mind, he was not working alone. Jeter's autonomy and success included a combination of independent and dependent thinking.

The need for autonomy is found in the mission of St. Joseph's Montessori School (SJMS) (St. Joseph's Montessori School 2023) in Columbus, Ohio. This school strives to prepare its graduates to be 21st century knowledge workers, defining the mindset needed for success as one of autonomy and learning:

SJMS' goals for its students include:

- *To foster a positive attitude toward learning*
- *To encourage self-confidence and independence*
- *To encourage an abiding curiosity*
- *To instill respect for the dignity of all humankind*

Collaboration and Team Engagement

Knowledge worker interactions demonstrate the importance of collaboration between subject-matter experts as described in *McKinsey Quarterly* (Johnson et al. 2005). As interactions increase, work productivity increases by 100 percent. Consider the implications of these findings as you cope with a continuously accelerating world and an increasing team environment. Collaboration is based on being able to identify your own expertise and the need for the expertise and contributions of others in their domains of expertise. A sense of autonomy positions you to be in control of a successful collaboration.

One last thought on 21st century knowledge work includes the increased focus on inclusivity and diversity. This focus is reported to also increase productivity. Knowledge workers are prepared to manage and maximize the various mindsets that come with inclusivity and diversity in the workforce to affect that increase in productivity. Clearly, increased productivity comes when you and others form a community mindset with all contributors.

Tom Brady, football quarterback of the Tampa Bay Buccaneers and previously of the New England Patriots, made it his priority to help the team come together and play with one goal in mind. He is a leader who has been recognized for his mindset of team community and its outcomes. Every team member is his customer as he mentors and encourages each of them. He holds each member accountable to be present in expediting his individually defined role and responsibility to the game. Brady led his team to 10 Super Bowl games with wins

in seven of these games. His outcomes are phenomenal, making him a
recognized GOAT, a greatest of all time!

Autonomy and learning are especially important when working within
a team, as the team's delivery is dependent upon the combined expertise
of all members. Members are integrating their individual knowledge for a
more informed outcome. Autonomy means that each member takes charge
(independence) of a contribution toward the common goal and has the
ability to integrate the contributions (dependence) of other members. They
are all stakeholders in the team effort. Work is not achieved by one person. Identifying, acknowledging, and leveraging the expertise and mindsets
of stakeholders, being anyone who can support or derail your work, are
essential activities. These stakeholders align mindsets to create a common
and collaborative path to a desired outcome. The 21st century knowledge
workers with learning mindsets continuously integrate different stakeholder
mindsets and knowledges into their own for optimal decision making.

The Importance of Narrative

Your narrative is your story. It describes how you believe, behave,
decide, and work. Checking on your narrative from both your own and
stakeholders' perspectives is a great way to determine the mindset that is
driving your activities. What story do you tell about yourself? Is it aligned
with the goals and values that you
define for yourself? What story do
your stakeholders tell about you?
Is it aligned with the story you tell

> **Is your narrative what you want it to be?**

about yourself? The following chapters will help you answer these questions so that you can be assured that your mindset is supporting the destiny you desire.

Learnability Quotient

Learnability is the desire and ability to routinely acknowledge and address
your weaknesses and strengths in order to ensure your growth and value
creation. The mindset that supports this desire and ability includes a focus
on growth, humility, and work ethic. Your learnability quotient (LQ)

(Coyle 2013) defines your capacity to seek clarity on any given topic to fuel this growth. It is a metric that is important in today's world. An autonomous worker will not meet success without a capacity for learning. Your mindset, others' mindsets, the environment, and extenuating circumstances provide context for your work. Learning in all of these areas creates readiness and guidance for directing your work.

Is one of your beliefs tainting what you research? What mindset component might impact your inquiry?

Your mindset impacts your learning as it influences your inquiry and subsequent research. Your goal, values, beliefs, and mode of work can slant your efforts. Mindset components shape your perspectives and, therefore, your learning. Understanding your mindset makes you aware of these formative perspectives and allows you to change them as needed. Mindset has a critical impact on your learnability quotient.

Damien was a very promising tennis player. He aspired to great victories. As a teenager, he had many friends and a lively social life, which he loved. But he knew that if his goal were to become a world-recognized athlete, he would have to focus his time and energy on tennis, not on his teenage social activities and friends. In light of this goal, he took up residence in a sports academy to facilitate that focus. He couldn't let himself be distracted by a social focus with his friends that would undoubtedly compromise his work toward his goal to achieve professional athletic status. His alignment of his goals, values, beliefs, and mode of work led him to his desired destiny.

Learning about one's mindset and, then, aligning the components with each other is essential to achieving your desired outcomes. It is worth observing how others allow their mindsets to limit their success with behaviors that do not align with their values or goals. For example, if you believe that all lively and loud sports' fans are foolhardy and short-term thinkers, you will most likely not consult a sports fan to collaborate with you on some longer-term and important goal, such as enhancing the value and availability of sports to disadvantaged children. A sports fan might be your best resource when researching this sports-related work.

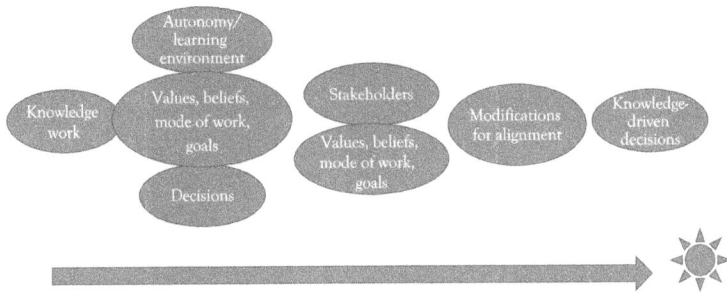

Figure 1.4 Knowledge work concept map

Discounting that person's input based on your belief doesn't serve you well. Your belief may have shut out some important and available information. Without even considering the input of the sports fan, you cannot reap the benefits of the fan's perspective on your work. Completely independent thought is not learning oriented and often discounts beneficial input, leading to actions that are harmful to your outcomes. Figure 1.4 summarizes the concept of knowledge work.

The learning mindset (Dweck 2016) is the key to your autonomy in the knowledge economy. There are two types of mindset: one of performance and one of learning. The performance mindset is focused on achieving a reward, a gold medal, or the completion of a task. Alter-

> **Do you seek to learn along with performing well?**

natively, the learning mindset is focused on learning that will ultimately support a performance goal. Everyone has both mindsets, as needed, but the learning mindset is more essential to long-term sustainability. Learners most effectively deal with the changes that the 21st century regularly imposes, but awareness of both mindsets will lead to a balance that will most effectively lead to your success. Figure 1.5 describes the performance and learning mindsets.

Success and Luck?

A lucky environment supports your successes (Frank 2016). Frank defines a lucky environment as being born into wealth or abundant resources to support your efforts and growth. Undeniably, these lucky environments create advantages. If this is not your situation, ask yourself how you might create a supportive environment for yourself. Taking

Carol Dweck, Mindset

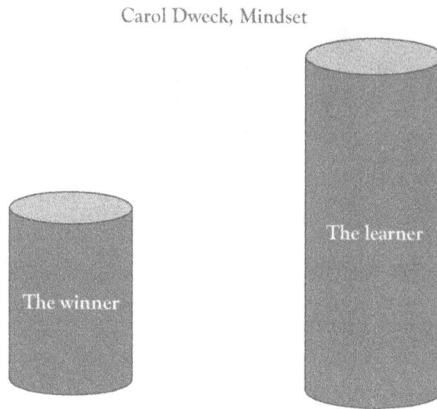

The learner

The winner

Figure 1.5 The mindset of learning

control, structuring learning, working with relevant people as mentors, and connecting to experts can create this lucky environment to support your success. Your strategic efforts replace the luck that Frank describes.

> *Wes Moore, author of* The Other Wes Moore *(2011), as a middle-school student in Baltimore was not on a good path. His mother created a lucky environment for him by sending him to a boarding school outside of his low-income neighborhood that was rampant with gangs, killings, and other crime. After a few escape attempts, Wes eventually aligned to his mother's efforts and began to create a mindset to achieve goals of self-sufficiency and success. After a very diverse and meaningful career, he was elected as Governor to the state of Maryland. Coincidentally, another young man named Wes Moore lived around the corner from the first Wes Moore. He didn't have or create a lucky environment for himself and is now serving a life sentence for murder.*

Creating a lucky environment means recognizing and taking advantage of your invisible capital (Raab 2010). Your invisible capital is all that you know and all the people you know because you have been alive for x number of years. Recognizing the value of this invisible capital is an essential part of your mindset.

Leaders in a community or organization can create this lucky environment by establishing the goals, values, beliefs, and mode of work that will support, reinforce, and reward autonomous work and decisions for success, both for individuals and for the community. They are creating an environment for success.

Philly Foodworks, when faced with significant growth challenges, created an environment that increased employee autonomy, building their abilities in decision making to propel the company through its challenges and manage for success.

New Economic Activity

Justin Trudeau, prime minister of Canada, stated in his address at the 2018 World Economic Forum, Davos, Switzerland: "The pace of change has never been this fast, yet it will never be this slow again."

General acceleration, a pandemic, and knowledge work create a new platform of economic activity. Upwork (Press Release December 15, 2020), the largest work marketplace, predicts that 22 percent of the American workforce will work remotely by 2025. This trend confirms the new and autonomous work needs of knowledge workers.

A recent report (McKinsey and Company 2021) notes eight trends and resulting changes that are reshaping the world economy and the world of work. They include:

Innovation: "The number of new patents being granted in the US is running at twice the levels we saw in 2019, and many other countries have also seen significant increases."

Consumer behavior: "We have seen ten years of digital innovation in roughly three months, and e-commerce across the globe has increased by two to five times from the levels prior to the pandemic." Web sales have increased from $3 trillion in 2016 to $4.29 trillion in 2020.

Environment: "Climate change is an existential risk, but it is also probably the biggest opportunity of our generation in terms of the scale and scope of investment needed to ensure the recovery is more green than brown." Expenditures for environmental protection for air, water, waste, land, and biodiversity have been significantly increasing from 2014 to 2019 (66 percent).

Health care: "There has been a healthcare revolution…in-person to telemedicine. Science is not standing still….$180B being spent on research to get us vaccines and other tools…180 times the level of prior pandemic investment."

Government scrutiny: "Throughout these crises, the government has become the lender, payer, and owner of last resort across a whole swath of industries. And with increased involvement comes increased government scrutiny…." Survey results report that "More U.S. adults want the government to have a bigger role in improving peoples' lives than before the pandemic….also found high support for universal health care, paid sick leave policies, and unemployment benefits."

Restructuring corporate portfolios: "Last year saw a significant shift in value, with the top quintile of companies gaining $240B of economic profit while the bottom 20 percent lost $400B." Venture capital investment returns rose from 19.8 percent in 2019 to 51.0 percent in 2020. U.S. private equity investment returns rose from 13.9 percent to 21.3 percent.

Shifting supply chains: "The past year highlighted the need for resilience. At the same time, you cannot change your supply chain overnight—in fact, fewer than 25 percent of all supply chains could relocate over five years—but we will nevertheless see changes in supply chains." Pandemic supply chains were impacted by changes in labor and buying patterns and impacted those patterns exponentially in reverse due to these same trends.

Returning to air travel: "Global traffic has fallen dramatically, and we expect it will not return to prior levels until 2024."

Other trends to consider are that corporate downsizing reduces the cost of real estate and automating administrative functions adds to the changes incurred by the pandemic.

Knowledge Worker Leaders and Managers

In addition to all of these trends, the uncertainty of the current global economy and the growing need for workers in the near future will foster an increasing need for employee commitment and loyalty (Chalofsky 2003). Supporting and motivating these employees is imperative. Leaders and managers have to have a plan for uncovering and meeting employee mindset needs.

> Ask yourself how these changes affect you and consider how you might better control these impacts. What mindset component will help you manage an impact? Do any of your mindset components need adjustment?

The Seven Skills of Autonomy

An autonomous mindset focuses on taking control, setting goals, and learning for good decision making. Recognizing the need to take control is the first step in being autonomous. Once you are committed to being in charge, goal setting and learning set a very logical path to being autonomous. The seven skills of autonomy include:

1. *Considers mindsets*: Knowledge workers consider the four components of mindset and their alignment to each other. Mindset considerations happen for each decision and for stakeholders involved in a work initiative.
2. *Sets goals and pursues results*: Knowledge workers set goals as part of their mindsets, including a hierarchy of incremental goals and results expected for each effort, including daily work.
3. *Values inquiry and learning*: Knowledge workers query on all efforts and define expected learning, including exploration of contributing mindsets in support of all efforts.
4. *Ensures data access and uses data for decisions*: Knowledge workers use a digital nervous system (Gates 1999) to support queries with relevant data and information for decision making.
5. *Makes decisions*: Knowledge workers are comfortable and competent in systematic and routine decision making.
6. *Reflects for generating new value ideas and celebrates new value*: Knowledge workers automatically reflect on all work, initiatives, and outcomes to improve performance and to identify new ideas and opportunities.

7. *Creates new value*: Knowledge workers systematically pursue improvements and opportunities to create benefits that positively impact themselves and/or their organizations.

An Autonomous Environment to Support Autonomous Skills

Knowledge worker's autonomous skills are not possible without an environment that supports them. Leaders and managers in 21st century organizations can ensure the value of autonomous knowledge work by building the following dimensions into their organizations:

1. Organizational mindset and narrative are defined and shared, including performance and learning goals and a standardized mode of work.

2. Mindset awareness and alignment are required and supported with relevant data and information for individuals, stakeholders, organizations, and partners.

3. A digital nervous system is available for data and information analysis and alignment of mindset, global and local trends and events, future-state potential opportunities, workflow and archetype forecasting, decision influencers, and choice architectures.

4. Confidence building, inquiry, and learning orientation are provided through a learning system structure that guides prior learning references, teams and projects, autonomous decision making, economic and mindset evaluation, archetype workflow analysis, and future state speculation.

5. Recognition and rewards are earned by new value creators/contributors and initiators sharing data on the contribution to the enterprise.

6. Intrapreneuring for new ideas is supported and reinforced by a Reflection for Growth (RFG) team.

7. Management theories of X, Y, and Z are balanced situationally, as needed, with personal profiles, satisfiers, and motivators to support individual and organizational growth initiatives.

Worksheet Reference

Worksheets to facilitate using the concepts in this chapter are found in "Developing the Intentional Mindset, Module 1: Understanding the Knowledge Economy." The worksheets include:

Your Knowledge Economy
Global Economy
Regional Economy
Local Economy
Assessing Your Autonomy
Assessing Your Organizational Autonomy

Chapter Summary

This chapter describes the 21st century knowledge economy and its new requirements for working with an autonomous mindset for decision making and control of one's destiny. The next chapter describes the components of a mindset and how to manage them for the best decision making.

CHAPTER 2

Defining Mindset Components

A small software company and a large hardware company decided to create a partnership to build out and offer a new line of products together. Managers

21st century insights and skills require awareness and management of mindset.

were assigned from both companies to work together, to build stakeholdership, and to design the product line using both sets of expertise. Defining a new offering that combined expertise was the easiest part of the partnership. They would not be successful unless they could agree on the mindset factors that would facilitate this work. Goals, values, beliefs, and mode of work had to make a common platform in order to effectively build joint products.

Smaller companies usually have a much less formal mode of work than larger companies. They have different decision protocols and communication strategies. They also have very different values to guide work. Some companies can be less focused on profit and more on market share. Others only want to be known for quality and not quantity. Still others are focused on owning intellectual rights to new offerings as opposed to sharing those rights with partners for better stakeholdership and market development. The mindset discussions didn't yield a common platform so the partnership ended in failure.

Mindsets happen automatically as you are born, learn, and live through experiences. They can also be intentionally created and used to guide your behaviors and decisions, as well as help you understand other's mindsets. Recognizing the components of your mindset allows you to control behaviors, activities, and decisions for working toward your destiny.

An unconscious mindset can derail all your hard work toward a goal or it can propel you to great success. Being aware of your mindset is key to being able to shape and control it. Let's delve into what mindset includes and how you might like to shape yours. Remember that it controls a large percentage of your decisions, whether good or bad.

Cognitive behavioral therapy is a form of psychological treatment to address thinking problems such as depression, anxiety, and eating disorders. This therapy addresses your manner of thinking or your mindset that can lead to dysfunctional behaviors. At the most basic level, the intent here is to merely help you understand how and what you think based on previous decisions. When you can confront this thinking, you can avoid less than helpful decision making in your future activities.

Mindsets can be an unconscious mind that is often below your level of awareness, even thought of as individual intuitions (Brooks 2012). They dictate your actions and decisions. In order to control that mindset, you can intentionally bring higher awareness of your mindset by defining it as your goals, values, beliefs, and mode of work. The definition, interaction, and alignment of these components is key to autonomous work that will meet your desired results.

This mindset also creates your narrative, which tells your story to the world, a story that you want to be sure to design yourself through the mindset you convey. Brooks (Brooks 2016) discusses your "resume virtues and eulogy virtues." Your narrative will include your work (resume) achievements and your personal (eulogy) characteristics. Both are important in building the story you want others to tell about you. And your mindset will structure how both narratives turn out. This makes understanding your mindset so very critical. Figure 2.1 shows the components of mindset.

> **Are you aware of your mindset and its message so that you can manage it?**

The components of mindsets include:

- **Goals**—describe what you intend to accomplish longer term (vision of destiny/legacy) and short term (mission or current projects) in service to personal, professional, community, and expertise aspirations; in the context of values.

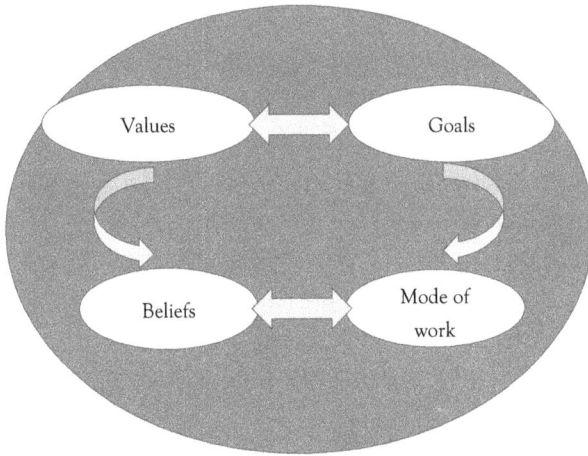

Figure 2.1 The making of a mindset

- **Values**—are the core principles by which you live life; in the context of your goals.
- **Beliefs**—are the opinions, assumptions, and biases that are prompted by your values and goals, pertain to a certain domain, event, activity, set of people, or industry, and so on.
- **Mode of work**—is the way you work that demonstrates and aligns to your goals, values, and beliefs.

When an outcome is not as positive as you might desire, it makes sense to examine the rationale for your actions and decisions that led to that outcome. Was the goal unrealistic or did your actions and decisions not align with your goal? Were your goals, values, beliefs, and mode of work able to support each other? If your goal isn't possible to achieve due to a value and subsequent belief, then your goal or your belief needs to be altered. All four mindset components need to support each other. This calls for mindset awareness and management.

Think Company (Starke 2022), founded in 2007, is a premier experience design and technology consulting company, helping businesses create great experiences for their customers and their employees. It is focused on enhancing people's lives by putting data insights into the hands of decision makers. Think Company workers, called Thinkers, study a client's need for improvement or a gap in its operations using evidence-based design and development. Thinkers identify all stake-holders, their involvement in the data need, and how they might (or might not) benefit from a digital solution to fulfill those needs. Think-ers create a project to determine and align the vision of all users and then design a solution to accommodate. Once the client and Thinkers have arrived at the same vision, the project work can be defined to begin fulfilling it. When aligned between client and Thinkers, that vision is considered the desired end state of the solution.

The key ideas in this chapter include:

- Mindset, destiny, and legacy
- Goals and results
- Values: core principles
- Beliefs, opinions, assumptions, biases
- Mode of work and stakeholders
- Integration and Alignment of Mindset Components

Mindset, Destiny, and Legacy

Mindset, what and how you think, is greatly overlooked as a determinant of your success. When you value something that is not aligned with a goal, that often leads to a negative outcome. When you believe in and work toward a

> **Can you define and align your mindset components to ensure your success?**

goal, outcomes can be better. This is not accidental, it is because beliefs, behaviors, and decisions align with your goals and values.

Let's explore each of the mind-set components in detail to see how they align with each other to guide thinking, behaviors, decisions, and destiny or legacy.

Goals and Results

Goals play a critical role as part of your mindset. They give you destinies or legacies to pursue. They enable you to achieve when you are confused or unsure of what to do next. They give you a frame of reference for making your work meaningful. You always benefit with a goal, even if you have to

Vision—Long-term destiny

⬇ ⬆

Mission—Today's outcomes toward destiny

⬇ ⬆

Projects—Today's work structures

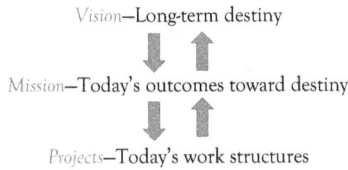

Figure 2.2 Vision, mission, and projects

modify it along the journey to achieving it. Goals can be personal, professional, community, or focused on individual expertise. And they will all reflect a vision and a mission. Vision represents the destiny you aspire to achieve long term. Mission represents the short-term projects and work you will pursue in order to achieve your vision, represented in Figure 2.2.

An all-important aspect of goals is the result that you expect to achieve. Sometimes referred to as outcomes, these results are most helpful when they are defined in tangible terms. Measures and metrics help to define exactly what the result or outcome should look like. Goals are important but cannot be effective if they don't include the results expected, as well as how they will be measured. The metric defines a target amount to be achieved and the measure defines how that metric will be tracked or measured. An outcome cannot be left to chance. Every goal needs a desired result to be complete, even when considering daily work. Success may be based on luck, but that lucky environment will often need to be designed and created based on the metrics that define the desired outcome.

When working with others it is often the common goal that enables people to work together effectively, especially when values, beliefs, and mode of work differ. Keeping in mind the common goal allows people to be more flexible in how they work and focus on what they will achieve together. Figure 2.3 describes comprehensive goal setting and structure.

Thinkers help clients align their mindsets through the visioning exercise (Starke 2013). This alignment toward a common vision brings all designers and users to a common understanding of the purpose and objective of their work, including an understanding of common values, beliefs, and mode of work. This vision guides the joint work and decisions of the client and the Thinkers as they research user needs and systematically build a solution to achieve the common goal of that vision.

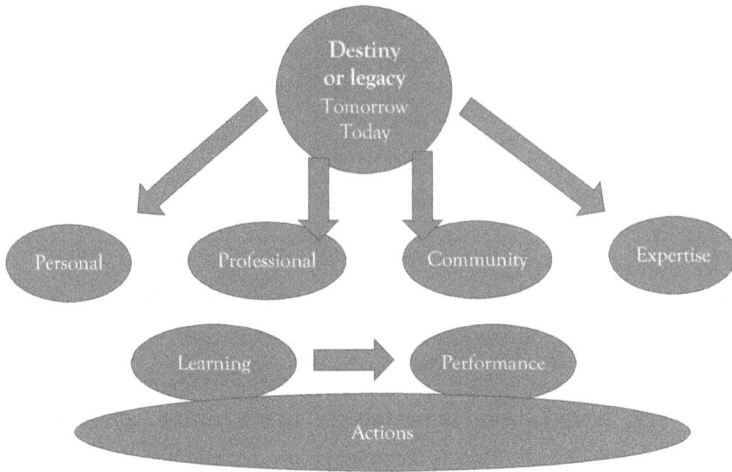

Figure 2.3 Comprehensive goal setting

*Thinkers' project strategy is to research to learn, build to imple-
ment, and test with feedback. They base their implementation steps on
research but still continuously test outcomes to evaluate expectations
and the effectiveness of solutions. The user needs, once aligned to the
common vision, are the driving force for evaluation and revisions.
Evaluations are done at every step of the project work.*

Goal Categories

Personal goals relate to your destiny and narrative as a person. Professional
goals give you context for work achievements or legacy. Community goals
define your contributions to your community. Expertise goals define your
subject-matter area of expertise and the level of competency you would
like to attain. Daily goals achieve the results you look for in the tasks of a
work session as they support the other longer-term goals.

Learning Versus Performance Goals

Sometimes goals are for learning and other times they are for a specific
outcome of tangible performance. Learning goals help you acquire data,
information, and knowledge that support achievement of performance
goals. These performance goals define what you actually need to achieve.
Everyone needs to have a balance of learning and performance goals.

Usually learning goals and performance goals can both support your vision and your mission's project work. In all cases, they work together to provide the certainty of a path to success.

Hierarchy of Goals

An important aspect of all work is the persistence needed to reach a goal. An incremental series of goals aligned with a higher-level goal builds persistence to persevere when obstacles or changes present challenges that must be overcome. Persistence (Duckworth 2018) is a key factor in achieving your destiny or legacy. Figure 2.4 relates project goals to vision.

A hierarchy of goals builds persistence and keeps focus on the vision and the mission simultaneously. The incremental goals of a

> **Do you have a hierarchy of personal or professional goals?**

hierarchy are focused on the mission or project goals that support the vision goal. This structure makes sure that work is aligned and ultimately working in the direction of the vision.

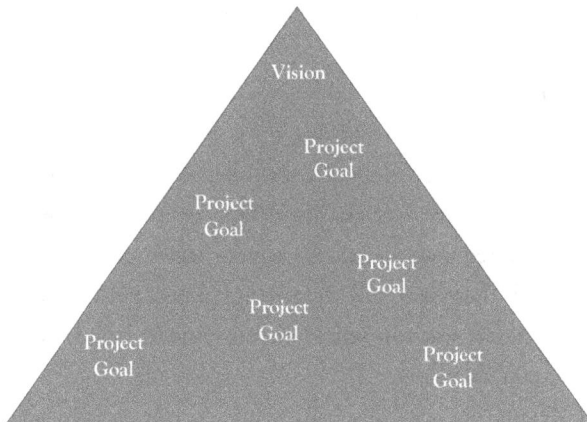

Figure 2.4 Vision, projects, hierarchy of goals

Daily Goals

Daily work should also be done in the context of a goal. This practice ensures that all work is aligned and contributing in the right direction to the higher goal it is intended to support. These goals may be the most important because they relate all work to the longer-term goals. Random and wasteful work doesn't happen when daily goals are intentionally set and pursued.

The global pandemic of 2020 (Fuhrmans and Weber 2021) introduced new work requirements to many high-profile workers. Most knowledge work, as well as school work, was relegated to the home. Those workers who had been focused on career goals and advancement were now working at home while supervising their children's school work. With these new conditions and the positivity they found in them, many of these people reprioritized their goals from career to family and changed jobs, as needed, to be able to focus on family for more of their time. Visions and missions were altered accordingly.

Values: Core Principles

Values are the core principles by which you live life. Values are at the heart and core of all thinking, goal creation, beliefs, mode of work, and decisions. They must be monitored as they relate to your decisions, destiny, and legacy.

Understanding values allows you to understand your motivations for decisions and outcomes. Do you value people over money? Sympathy over helpfulness? Dependence over independence? Health over fun? Safety over risk? Quality over quantity? Time over friendship? These values can be uncovered with an analysis of your recent decisions and behaviors. They tell all there is to tell about your values. How do you actually identify your values? Ask yourself what you value or look for evidence on what you actually do value.

Now try exploring how your values impact your life. One can explore this connection by analyzing behaviors and decisions and the outcomes they have caused. How are those behaviors and decisions aligned with your stated values? This exploration ultimately helps you identify actual values and not those you think you have. Values can be implicit and unconscious but your behaviors and decisions tell the real truth about what you value. Behaviors and decisions lead to outcomes. Do your outcomes surprise you or are they as expected? Do you need to reexamine what you actually value? And do your values align with the other components of your mindset? Conflicts here will cause confusion and less-than-helpful decisions.

As new working modes of collaboration and autonomy evolve in the 21st century, your values also need to be aligned with stakeholders' values. What values do you share with your stakeholders? Do you need to alter your values or help your stakeholders alter theirs?

Think Company Thinkers aren't satisfied with a project until outcomes are overwhelmingly accepted as successful. These outcomes are defined and guided by the vision and mission goals at the beginning of the project. Further, Thinkers and the clients have to work from the same values in order to determine a project's success. Goals and values are linked to each other, as well as aligned among all stakeholders.

You might create your values based on what you want to achieve, as well. Values and goals evolve together. Values determine what is important to you. Is it winning a prize, gaining recognition, or continuous learning toward a better future outcome? Values drive your beliefs, mode of work, and decisions. Values can be tied to your project needs, those of your stakeholders or community, or your goals for a desired legacy. They are important as they impact so many aspects of your life.

In essence, a goal becomes a value and a value becomes a goal. So, it is less important what comes first, your values or your goals. It is more important that they match so that they are not conflicting with each other in guiding your work. If an outcome is less than desirable, check your values to see if they need some altering or maybe it is a goal

> **How do your goals and values align with each other?**

that needs refinement. Check your goals to see if they can be altered to redirect your values. In all cases, make sure that your stated goals and values are real and defining a common path as they advise your work. Does your work reflect your values and goals?

Values Tool Inventory

A few sample values inventories are listed in the following. This inventory of tools is not exhaustive but does support contemplation of your own values and beliefs. They include examples of what others have identified as values. Each item could have a different meaning to different individuals, so use your imagination in thinking about their meanings in the context of you and your life's goals, and add others as they seem relevant to your life.

A **Life Values Inventory** (Brown and Crace 1996) includes:

- Achievement
- Belonging
- Concern for the environment
- Concern for others
- Creativity
- Financial prosperity
- Health and activity
- Humility
- Independence
- Loyalty to family or group
- Privacy
- Responsibility
- Scientific understanding
- Spirituality

A **Global Learning Value Rubric** (Association of American Colleges and Universities 2009) evaluates global learning and includes:

- Global self-awareness
- Perspective-taking
- Understanding of cultural diversity
- Personal and social responsibility
- Global systems and knowledge application of integrating systems

World Value Survey (World Value Survey, World Values Association 1981). Inglehart and Welzel created this survey to identify characteristics of culture, gender, religion, and happiness/life satisfaction. They used two scales:

- Survival versus self-expression
- Traditional (religion, etc.) versus secular perspectives

On these scales, they evaluated economic development, emergence and flourishing of democratic impact, rise of gender equality, and the extent of effective government. They found that poorer countries had values based on the need for survival and traditional life perspectives. Richer countries had more focus on self-expression and secular perspectives. This information provides insight for policymakers when building societies and democratic institutions in developing countries.

The **Benefits Events Values Inventory** (Shealy 2016) is an analytic tool that collects data on background, experiences, life events, beliefs, and values in order

> **How did you answer a recent challenger in an argument? What goal or value drove that answer?**

to adequately address these as context when working with a stakeholder. These components of a mindset are important when planning joint work with your stakeholders. Visit www.thebevi.com for information on using the benefits, events, values inventory (bevi tool).

Beliefs/Opinions/Assumptions/Biases

Beliefs are a subset of your values. Beliefs are your opinions, assumptions, or biases regarding the specifics of an issue, environment, group of people, or project. Beliefs translate your values into behaviors and decisions. And as values and goals are so closely related, these beliefs must also be aligned to support your goals. For example, if your goal is to reduce poverty, you might place value on reducing illiteracy, but a belief that some people don't need to learn to read would prompt behaviors that are not aligned with your goal or value. A belief that everyone should be able to read would better support your goal and value of reducing poverty with increasing literacy.

As tenets of your values, beliefs/biases can ensure that your values are applied to all of your work and decisions. You cannot align the value of complete communication with the belief that workers only need limited information to complete their tasks. When beliefs conflict with your stated values, behaviors do not lead to your goals. In this case, workers will not be able to complete tasks effectively if information is not readily available, derailing the value that would lead to goal attainment.

Beliefs can be implicit biases, which unconsciously skew your behaviors and decisions away from objectivity. Implicit biases are beliefs that are stereotypical, unconscious, and often misdirect a behavior or decision inadvertently. Do you seek the advice of a man before a woman, even if the woman is more qualified? Are you suspicious of a person who looks different from you, even though that person comes highly recommended? Do you gravitate toward a tall person instead of a short one for directions, even when the short person is from the neighborhood? Do you find more credibility in a person's opinion when you know that person better than you know another team member and his opinion? Is a Harvard graduate smarter than a Princeton graduate since you are a Harvard graduate?

Think Company Thinkers start their design process by defining the vision of the client with a narrative of the future, including longer-term and supporting smaller goals. This step identifies the biases that tend to predefine a solution based on client's and Thinkers' preconceived notions (beliefs). Once identified, beliefs/biases have to be reconciled and aligned to create a common vision. The client and Thinkers spend a significant amount of time together ensuring that the vision is free of biases that could taint the decisions and work to arrive at a commonly valued solution. Once the vision is established, the design work shifts to pain points, wants, needs, and workflow difficulties. These elements are the essential drivers of their collaborative project work that is defined in their project charter. The vision is used to continuously check on progress toward the smaller goals and, ultimately, the longer-term goal of the vision.

In the 21st century with high levels of collaboration needed, you often encounter implicit biases. Acceleration of everything pushes knowledge workers to make quick decisions, so evaluation of a situation is often made according to stereotypical and implicit bias. Beliefs as opinions, assumptions, and biases without inquiry can mislead the decision maker with subjective, nonfactual, and potentially false information. Beliefs should be checked to align with values and goals so that they guide behaviors and decisions accordingly. If you value a balance of power when collaborating, what behavior would demonstrate that value? Perhaps you try to make decisions together with your peers? Share perspectives prior to decision making? Create a decision protocol for ensuring a balance in thinking? Beliefs as opinions, assumptions, or biases can be obstacles when not aligned with a value or goal.

The outcome of the 2020 U.S. presidential election was mired in diverse goals, values, beliefs, and behaviors. The incumbent candidate was highly valued by a constituency of followers. He lost the election. His followers believed that the election was tainted by a compromised voting system. Their goal was to overturn the election. Others' value in the credibility of the voting system led to their belief that the election result was valid. These discrepancies of values and beliefs led to chaos, a disastrous event, and harm to law enforcement personnel. Values were diverse and so were beliefs that supported them.

You might consider your individual values as they compare to your leader's values. Is there conflict or do values align for best and collaborative decision making?

> **What recent opinion did you share in a discussion? What belief did it demonstrate? What value supported that belief?**

Beliefs Inventory

Beliefs are ultra-important because they lead to your mode of work, which directly builds your narrative. Beliefs must be true to your values if you want your behaviors and mode of work to build a credible narrative that tells your story.

A sample inventory of possible behaviors originating with your beliefs, opinions, assumptions, and biases includes:

- Sharing opinions and support of current events, as influenced by a friend's opinion
- Seeking confirmation of an opinion with selected research of facts, influenced by a desire to prove yourself correct
- Quantifying and qualifying diverse peoples, originating in some stereotypical anecdotes
- Tendency to feel compromised by others' actions, based on a lack of self-confidence
- Prioritizing money over all other interests, motivated by a lack of financial stability
- Being kind no matter how you are treated, based on a belief in nurturing others.
- Giving someone the benefit of doubt when others are critical of bad behavior
- Judging another's behavior without seeking to understand, instigated by a previously hurtful experience
- Excusing or rationalizing behaviors, instigated by a friendship with a person and need for approval

When beliefs are realistically recognized, their consequences can be forecasted, minimized, or maximized for the best outcomes possible. This is true for yourself, for others, and for collaborative work efforts.

Think Company was often confronted with a client perspective or value that was not demonstrated in their project requests. The Thinkers had to explore behaviors and beliefs with that client to agree on actual values by which work would be completed. Lack of clarity on values would derail work and render it unsatisfactory.

Aligning your values, goals, and beliefs is the first step in building behaviors and decisions for success. Can a goal to maximize revenue be supported by a value on eradicating poverty? How might this happen?

Understanding Modes of Work and Stakeholders

Understanding how you work, as well as how that work affects your outcomes and stakeholders, allows you to adjust or build a work mode to align with your goals, values, and beliefs for success.

How do you like to work? How do you communicate? Who makes decisions? What are the timeframes for getting to a result? Is the result or the process more important? How are others impacted by your mode of work? How are you impacted by theirs?

This list of questions on how you work could go on and on. How you choose to work, communicate, make decisions, and so on, is often not really consciously decided but guided by your beliefs. It is unconscious not only to yourself but also to a stakeholder or a team. When you work alone, your mode of work still needs to consider the receivers of that work. When you work with others, you need to consciously consider the receivers and collaborators, as well. When your mode of work is understood and aligned, progress is not delayed. It is best to plan a common understanding of your mode of work to communicate, track, and organize expectations effectively.

Thinkers were very focused on understanding their clients' mode of work so that they can match it with complementary services. Work on a common goal can be derailed if the mode of work is not conducive to both parties' expectations.

Individuals and organizations both have modes of work. It is most efficient when each party is aware of the other and can align their modes to avoid obstacles in expectations or actual collaboration. Modes of work can be a choice. Choose wisely to expedite progress.

Modes of work are usually guided by beliefs and they lead to your narrative. Designing a

Do your stakeholders' modes of work give you insight into your own modes of work?

mode of work takes great awareness of your own and other's mindset needs. How will you accommodate in order to work together effectively? What is the narrative you want to convey about yourself with this work?

Examples of Modes of Work

A sampling of modes of work for building an autonomous work environment is described in the following sections. It is important that these modes of work are set up and reinforced within an autonomous organization so that knowledge workers are aware of expectations on how work is done and feel supported in their endeavors. Individual modes and organizational modes are both described as they complement and impact each other and cannot be considered separately. There are additional modes of work presented in Chapter 4 "Behavioral Concepts and Examples" that are also valid and helpful considerations when seeking autonomy and learning.

Mode 1: Mindset Awareness

Social Intelligence (Goleman 2006) discusses how a mindset is communicated to another. It is demonstrated through your facial expressions that are caused by neural connections. The mindset that you convey when communicating is then mirrored in the reaction of your colleague, as well. This is called a neural mirror. If the person asking a question or delivering a directive is smiling and happy, then the receiver of this communication will mirror that expression in response. The response, however, may or may not be valid. Checking for true mindset is essential. When arguing a point in a debate, it is helpful to look for clues as to what your opponent really thinks. Body language? Neural mirrors? Words chosen? Contextual examples used?

These neural mirrors have been identified in psychological research as the ability to impact someone's response to you with the expression of your own feelings. When everyone is acting as a leader or decision maker in an autonomous environment, then everyone has the ability to convey a feeling to a listener or collaborator. Neural mirrors, how you communicate your thoughts and feelings with facial expressions and body language, impact your stakeholders and environment. Conversely, your reaction to a situation or another's thought can prompt your immediate reaction to mirror the mindset of a communicator. Are you aware of the positivity or negativity of your reactions, both as communicator and/or receiver of a communication?

Mode 2: Learning: Context, Inquiry, Enabler to All Autonomous Work

Learning is important as a value (Dweck 2016). Learning enables you to dissect and manage changes as they present themselves. Learning guides you to a better understanding of the change, its stakeholders, and its needs when integrating into your current existence.

Learning also enables you to explore your actual versus your intended and articulated mindset. This, then, enables you to use true values and beliefs to guide your actions and decisions. Learning also allows you to explore others' mindsets and likely decisions to align thinking and work.

When confronted with a dilemma, your choice can be adaptive or generative. The exploration of learning can lead to your decision to adapt yourself or generate a new solution to the dilemma. A status quo or adaptive decision might be the best solution to a change but only after seeking clarity to determine if this is, actually, the best solution. As automatic status quo decisions have their risks, learning can validate them as the best course of action. Conversely, generating a new solution can happen with an analysis of the situation, the stakeholders involved, and their needs.

Another aspect of learning centers on goal creation. As goals are set, it is important to understand the significance of learning goals. Is your goal focused on learning and what is the outcome of that learning? Often learning goals are incremental in nature, they are intended to lead to some other goal, which might be focused on performance, such as a win in a competition or completion of a project by a deadline. Learning goals are more focused on the process of building the competency needed to attain that other performance goal in the future. When you value learning, along with performance, you believe and practice inquiry in support of learning. Figure 2.5 demonstrates the connection between learning and performance.

Dweck explains how the learning mindset enables people to develop and grow and not focus solely on performance. Trying something new, even when you are unsure of the outcome, can lead to learning. If you don't try something because of a fear of potential failure, nothing is gained. Neither performance nor learning have been achieved in this case.

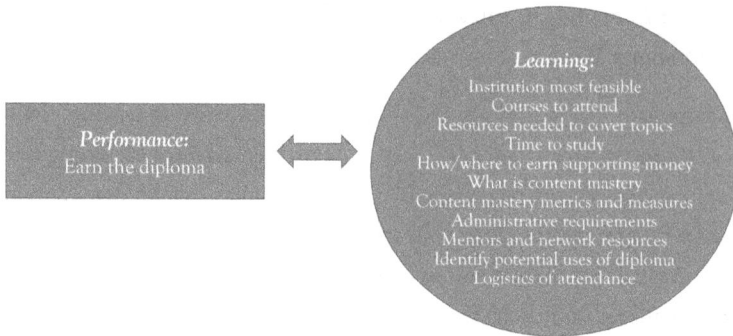

Figure 2.5 Connecting learning and performance

The primary value to embrace in the 21st century is that of learning. In today's dynamic knowledge economy, it is essential to be open to change. This involves learning as a routine and regular practice of inquiry, research, economic and mindset evaluation, problem solving, reinforcement, and reflection on outcomes. Most importantly, learning about your mindset allows you to manage its impact on decisions for the best outcomes that you define for yourself.

If a mother believes that pets are dangerous and should be feared, then her children may always be fearful and never have a pet. The art and practice of inquiry and learning helps you to consider the validity of your beliefs, especially when that belief presents an obstacle to a decision that might yield a positive outcome.

There is no question that opportunities are ubiquitous in the 21st century environment, but also extremely challenging since mindsets are so diverse. Learning is the art of thinking in ways that are open to change. Many factors can prompt integration of ideas and change if you are open to considering new opportunities, economic feasibility, and the mindsets of yourself and others.

Abraham Lincoln (Goodwin 2006), as the 16th President of the United States of America, was a champion of learning. When elected, he engaged his rival candidates to serve in cabinet positions. Lincoln wanted to understand and learn from their diverse mindsets and expertise. He is famous for his statement, "I don't like that man, I should get to know him better."

Fred Smith, Founder and CEO of FedEx, read a famous person's biography weekly to learn of success and failures. He didn't want to repeat others' mistakes and, also, wanted to benefit from their successes.

When you disagree with another, inquiry into the mindset that led to the diverse behavior or decision brings clarity and a potential path forward for the disagreeing parties. Uncovering differing mindsets can also lead to other aspects of the mindset that are aligned and, thus, an opportunity to prompt a common platform for alignment. Even when collaborators work differently in some ways, they may work similarly in other ways. Identifying common mindsets and work is a value of learning.

Mode 3: Being Autonomous in Work and Decision Making

An autonomous worker is in control by using an independent, yet dependent, mode of work. This autonomy is built with an awareness and management of oneself. *Managing Oneself* (Drucker 1999) notes that you should be aware of and take responsibility for your own strengths, values, and mode of work. These characteristics are the foundation for your mindset, development, and growth.

> **Do you manage your mindset to intentionally build your autonomy?**

How do you use your strengths and values to define your goals, beliefs, and mode of work? Growth and autonomy are most easily achieved by taking responsibility for Drucker's three characteristics.

Mode 4: Recognizing and Building Trust With Stakeholders

When organizing work with stakeholders, it is important to consider your mode of work. How you choose to work, communicate, make decisions, and so on, is often unknown to a stakeholder. It is best to consider and match modes of work with your stakeholders' modes. Collaborating on how you will work with others matches modes of work and eliminates a lot of unnecessary conflict along the journey to a successful outcome. This collaboration builds trust and relationship so that even when conflicts occur, they are minimal and easily overcome. Figure 2.6 describes a stakeholder framework for collaborative work.

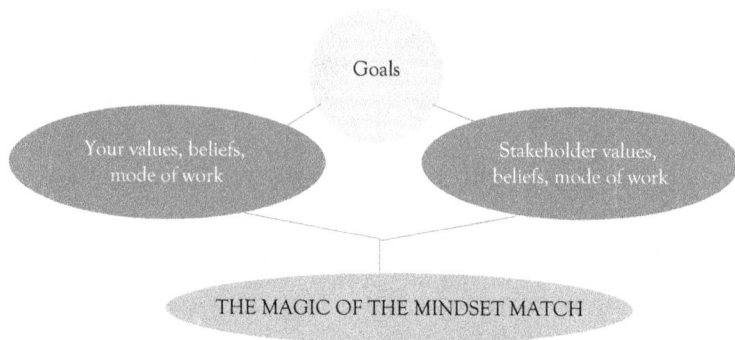

Figure 2.6 Essential stakeholder framework

Communications to initiate trust and relationship are important. Several conversation starters (Brooks 2020) can be used to build trust and relationship. Humans need to be heard before they can listen to another perspective. These conversation starters set up listening that conveys genuine interest and builds relationship. They are quoted as follows:

- **Approach with awe.** C. S. Lewis once wrote that if you'd never met a human and suddenly encountered one, you'd be inclined to worship this creature. Every human being is a miracle, and your superior in some way. The people who have great conversations walk into the room expecting to be delighted by you and make you feel the beam of their affection and respect. Lady Randolph Churchill once said that when sitting next to the statesman William Gladstone she thought him to be the cleverest person in England, but when she sat next to Benjamin Disraeli she thought she was the cleverest person in England.
- **Ask elevating questions.** All of us have developed a way of being that is our technique for getting through each day. But some questions, startling as they seem at first, compel us to see ourselves from a higher vantage: What crossroads are you at? What commitments have you made that you no longer believe in? Who do you feel most grateful to have in your life? What problem did you use to have but now have licked? In what ways are you sliding backward? What would you do if you weren't afraid?

- **Ask open-ended questions.** Many of us have a horrible tendency to ask questions that imply judgment: Where did you go to school? Or we ask yes/no questions: Did you have a good day? Which basically shut off interesting answers. Better questions start with "What was it like. ..." or "Tell me about a time. ..." or "How did you manage to cope while your wedding was postponed for a year?"

- **Make them authors, not witnesses.** The important part of people's lives is not what happened to them, but how they experienced what happened to them. So many of the best conversations are not just a recitation of events. They involve going over and over an event, seeing it from wider perspectives coating it with new layers of emotion, transforming it, so that, say, an event that was very hard to live through is now very satisfying to remember.

- **Treat attention as all or nothing.** Of course, we all have divided attention. In "You're Not Listening," Kate Murphy writes that introverts have more divided attention than others while in conversation because there's so much busyness going on in their own heads. But in conversation it's best to act as if attention had an on/off switch with no dimmer. Total focus. I have a friend who listens to conversations the way congregants listen to sermons in charismatic churches—with amens, and approbations. The effect is magnetic.

- **Don't fear the pause.** Most of us stop listening to a comment about halfway through so we can be ready with a response. In Japan, Murphy writes, "businesspeople are more likely to hear the whole comment and then pause, sometimes eight seconds, before responding, which is twice as long a silence as American business people conventionally tolerate."

- **Keep the gem statement front and center.** In the midst of many difficult conversations, there is what the mediator Adar Cohen calls the gem statement. This is the comment that keeps the relationship together: "Even when we can't agree on Dad's medical care, I've never doubted your good intentions.

I know you want the best for him." If you can both seize that gem statement it may point to a solution.

- **Find the disagreement under the disagreement.** In the Talmudic tradition, when two people disagree about something, it's because there is some deeper philosophical or moral disagreement undergirding it. Conversation then becomes a shared process of trying to dig down to the underlying disagreement and then the underlying disagreement below that. There is no end. Conflict creates cooperative effort. As neuroscientist Lisa Feldman Barrett writes, "Being curious about your friend's experience is more important than being right."

- **The midwife model.** Sometimes people talk to solve a person's problem. The Rev. Margaret Guenther wrote that a good conversationalist in these cases is like a midwife, helping the other person give birth to her own child. That means spending a lot of time patiently listening to the other person teach herself through her narration, bringing forth her unthought thoughts, sitting with an issue as it slowly changes under the pressure of joint attention. "To influence actions," neuroscientist Tali Sharot writes, "you need to give people a sense of control."

> **How do you use conversations to identify the mindsets of others?**

Mode 5: Inquiry—Five Whys and Seven Levels of Thinking

An approach for identifying mindsets is the *Five Whys* (Serrat 2009), in which you inquire *why* sequentially five times to identify a rationale for a behavior or decision. This method draws out the goal, value, beliefs, or mode of work that underlie a behavior or decision. Is the response to each of the *Five Whys* a fact or an opinion? Facts or opinions are further supported by the seven levels of inquiry and thinking of Bloom's taxonomy.

The exercise in Figure 2.7 suggests how to identify a rationale or an obstacle.

Why decision?

Decision to outcome =
Beliefs and mode of work

Why that decision?

Why that decision?

Why that decision?

Why belief supports?

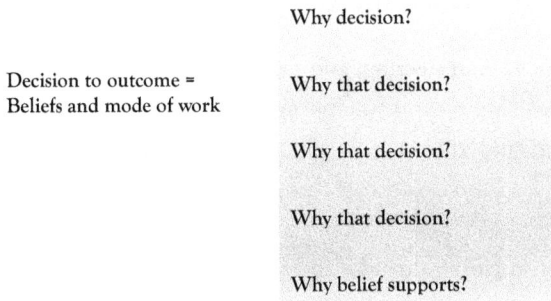

Figure 2.7 Five Whys triggers to beliefs and decisions

Bloom's (Armstrong 2010) inquiry levels can eliminate biases of opinions and assumptions from your thinking. The inquiries progress from identifying simple facts to deeper levels of inquiry that suggest new value creation. These levels of thinking are a substantial platform for intrapreneurial and entrepreneurial activity. Blooms' levels of inquiry include:

1. **Facts:** Build awareness and identification of basic facts and concepts.
2. **Understanding:** Explain why facts and/or concepts are important or relevant, background including characteristics, and connections between/among the facts and concepts.
3. **Application:** Use facts and/or concepts as they apply to new situations.
4. **Analysis:** Consider facts and concepts to identify individual meanings.
5. **Synthesis:** Consider facts, concepts, and their individual meanings as they might create a system for new and interdependent meaning to potentially create new value.
6. **Evaluation:** Consider the cost, benefits, and value of any new idea, be able to justify with economic and emotional analysis.
7. **Creation:** Produce new and original work or value through design and development.

When planning a new venture, *Five Whys* analysis, supported by the seven levels of inquiry, should give you a detailed and accurate description of the feasibility of the new venture.

Mode 6: Brainstorming, Brainsteering, Mind Mapping

Brainstorming, brainsteering, and mind mapping are helpful techniques that uncover connections among events, trends, scenarios, economies, stakeholders, and their needs. These techniques suggest new ideas or opportunities. They are described as follows:

- **Brainstorming** includes a very wide consideration and analysis of current events, trends, customers, and operations, such as global evolution. Figure 2.8 describes a brainstorming session.
- **Brainsteering** includes a narrower consideration and analysis of a specific domain of events, trends, customers, and operations, such as inflationary, education, or housing challenges. Figure 2.9 describes a brainsteering session.
- **Mind mapping** includes a compilation of brainstorming and/ or brainsteering outcomes into a refined map of connections to uncover cause and effect and opportunities. Figure 2.10 describes a mind mapping session.

When a competitor starts to overtake your customers and market, brainsteering on the specific stakeholders and externalities of the situation and mind mapping for helpful connections will lend insight into the cause and some possible solutions to the situation.

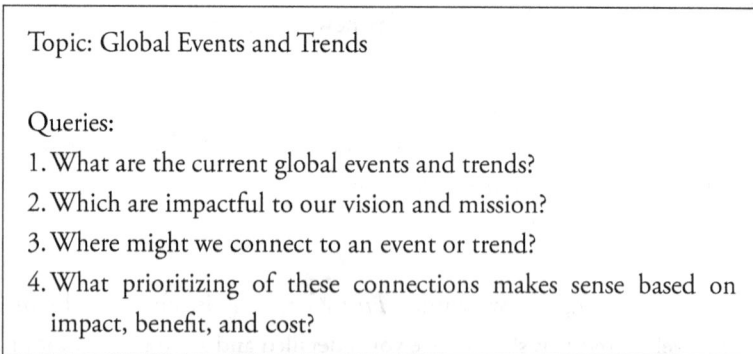

Topic: Global Events and Trends

Queries:
1. What are the current global events and trends?
2. Which are impactful to our vision and mission?
3. Where might we connect to an event or trend?
4. What prioritizing of these connections makes sense based on impact, benefit, and cost?

Figure 2.8 Brainstorming

Topic: Supply Chain Obstacles

Queries:
1. What are the supply chain obstacles?
2. Which are impactful to our vision and mission?
3. Where might we contribute to an impact?
4. What prioritizing of these contributions makes sense based on impact, benefit, and cost?

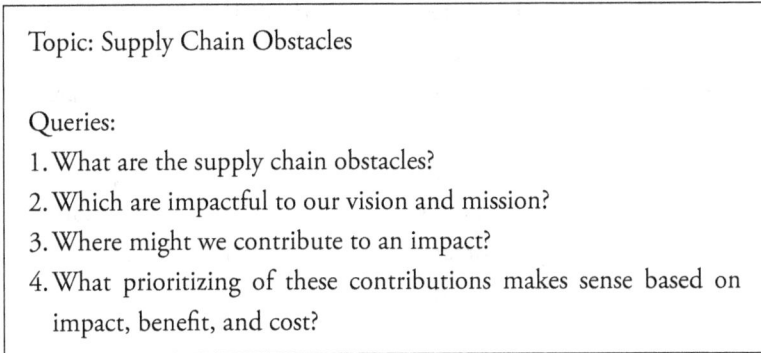

Figure 2.9 Brainsteering

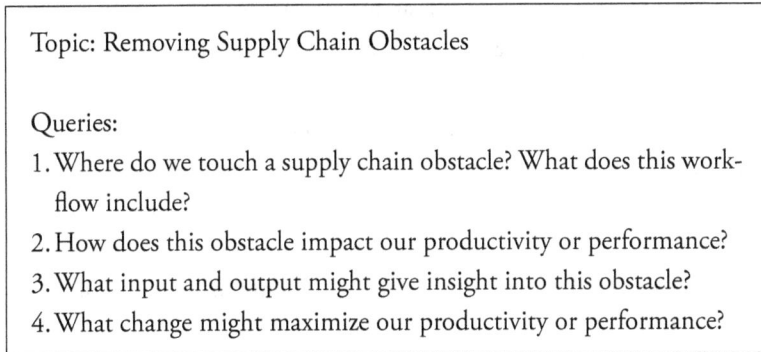

Topic: Removing Supply Chain Obstacles

Queries:
1. Where do we touch a supply chain obstacle? What does this workflow include?
2. How does this obstacle impact our productivity or performance?
3. What input and output might give insight into this obstacle?
4. What change might maximize our productivity or performance?

Figure 2.10 Mind mapping

Mode 7: Building the Artifacts of an Intentional Narrative, Individual and Organizational

Narratology, the study of stories, is an interesting field to explore. Stories are often more meaningful than a factual description of a person or organization. They tell of a real situation, representing reality that resonates with listeners. People depend on the reality they gain from the story. Stories capture the listeners attention in a way that is meaningful and remembered (Mitra 2017). They automatically feel trust and relationship because they see themselves or a loved one in the story.

A narrative (Shiller 2019) is a story that is believed because it is talked about over and over again. This recurring message about you or your organization is told through the artifacts that you create through behaviors, mode of work, and decisions that represent your goals and values. These artifacts are the proof of you or your organization and they earn trust in you.

People have narratives and organizations have narratives. They are the best indicators of the mindsets of people involved and how work gets done, giving great insight into the potential future of working with others. Also, consider how closely your individual mindset or narrative is aligned with that of your organization. If not aligned, conflicts will be many and frustration will be a daily occurrence.

Your story or your narrative can be positive or it can be detrimental to your work. When others have a narrative about you, they will act in the context of that story. It is your responsibility to ensure that your narrative conveys an accurate and desirable picture. Is your current mindset building the narrative that you desire? Is it supporting your success or derailing it?

An artifact can include listening to all points of view to build a narrative that you are open to considering changes to current activity. Another artifact might be recognizing another's excellent work to show that you appreciate others' endeavors and are not only focused on your own work.

> **Have you checked your narrative lately?**

Think Company calls its workers Thinkers. This is an artifact that defines work as based on inquiry, evaluation, and learning. Thinking is not a status quo activity. It presumes learning.

Mode 8: Use of a Digital Nervous System

A digital nervous system (Gates 1999) is a framework of basic data and information about an organization's operations, sales, customers, competitors, trends, industry, market, strategy, vision, and members. When you structure the right questions for inquiry through the *Five Whys* or the seven levels of inquiry and thinking, it is essential to support these questions with relevant data and information. The digital nervous system of data and information allows you to glean answers and can also support new questions based on these answers. Often secondary questions suggest how data and information can be pivoted for additional insight into a situation. Why did an outcome happen? *Why* did that happen? *Why? Why? Why?* And *Why?* The digital nervous system supports these inquiries.

When data statistics present alarming information on your market situation, the next logical question of *Why?* suggests a new question and view of data and information to answer it.

Mode 9: High- and Low-Level Reactions

Human brains have a dual-response system (Kahneman 2011). System One responses are low-level and unconscious, immediate, and reactionary. They happen often in an emergency when time to think is not available and a reaction is necessary to secure safety or to avoid a drastic hazard. System Two responses are high-level and conscious, more delayed, and take time to reflect on an appropriate response. They happen when there is time for consideration of the pros and cons of a situation. Both are valid responses, depending on the needs of a specific situation. Being aware and in control of these reactions as much as possible is the best approach for decision making and for positive outcomes. How do you respond to a dilemma?

> **What triggers cause System One or System Two thinking for you?**

If your car is on fire, a System One response is probably the best course of action. If you are choosing a new pair of shoes, System Two will best help you decide.

Mode 10: Multiple Intelligences for Learning

People have different kinds of intelligences (Gardner 1993) and, therefore, learn in different ways. These intelligences include visual, linguistic, interpersonal, intrapersonal, logical, musical, kinesthetic, and naturalistic tendencies. Understanding your own intelligence, as well as those of your stakeholders, is helpful in identifying and matching mindsets for best outcomes. A person who is very linguistically-oriented will make different decisions than a person who is kinesthetically-oriented. The linguistically-oriented person will relate to the written word while the kinesthetically-oriented person will be more physically-oriented in their behaviors. These structures will influence thinking and decisions, and can be maximized situationally for best outcomes. This approach also enhances worker self-confidence and motivation.

How do you learn? Do you learn visually? Through audio, tactile modes, words, or comparisons? How you learn will dictate your inquiry and sharing of data and information, so it is important to know this about yourself and others as your stakeholders.

Understanding how you and others learn can drastically impact how and what you communicate and how others can relate to your sharing of knowledge and/or learnings. Matching learning modes with the mode of information presented is essential for engagement.

> **Do you know your best learning mode?**

Using music to convey a concept will be engaging for children who are too young to read. Using numbers to make a point or change another's perspective might be a good choice for a group of economists.

Mode 11: Communication Plan Models

> **Can you identify your specific communication with any of these techniques?**

A definitive communication plan (Jensen 2000) integrates stakeholders' perspectives into your communication. It strives to develop trust with relevant communication that considers the mindset of others. His structure is described in Table 2.1 and includes four areas to consider.

Table 2.1 Jensen communications plan

1. **Intent**—What do you want stakeholders to do with your message? How will you measure this stakeholder activity? Where do you want them to arrive in their thinking?
2. **Content**—How will your message facilitate your intent, getting your stakeholders to complete the activity that you want?
3. **Format**—How, when, and where will you deliver your message and value statement for best results? Consider how to motivate your stakeholders.
4. **Context**—How is your communication/message relevant to each stakeholder? Where is each in his current thinking?

Talking to a colleague about another's success will not motivate a commitment since context and circumstances are most likely not the same for these two people.

Mode 12: Persistence

Persistence (Duckworth 2016) is critical as a mode of work. This persistence can be established and supported in your passion. Having an ultimate goal and a hierarchy of goals to support your continued efforts keeps you on a persistent track to follow your passion. Persistence is intentional, planned, and tracked as progress mounts toward the goal of your passion.

Don Sutton is a unique baseball hall of famer (Kepner 2021). Sutton never had a "win it all" record but earned very high statistics for his playing years. He attributes this record to his farming upbringing where a dedication to the job was of upmost importance and became a persistent mode of work and life. One had to be "all in" no matter the weather conditions or economic returns. It was a job and deserved the passion of total commitment. Sutton transferred this "all in" dedication to his career with his approach to playing the game. He was persistent in dedication to playing the game for the best outcome, not to a team or another person. His passion was his consistent commitment to his life's work, which happened to be baseball at the time.

Using a hierarchy of goals facilitates your persistence to achieve your ultimate vision or goal. Cel-

> **How do you build persistence into your work?**

ebration of each milestone can reinforce the efforts necessary for that achievement and spark energy for achieving the next milestone. Creating a series of goals arranged in a hierarchy is Duckworth's idea of persistence.

A young woman who aspired to become a medical doctor created a hierarchy of goals regarding her science education. She made this hierarchy of goals in middle school and continued to achieve through high school, college, and medical school. She achieved her dream of serving others' medical needs as an acclaimed pediatrician.

Mode 13: Project Thinking

Project thinking uses structures to keep work on track. Planning and setting up work in a way that keeps you engaged and progressing sequentially through incremental steps to the goal is a formula for achievement. This strategy also provides a common platform for collaborative work efforts to complement each other and stay on track as a team effort. Project thinking includes a charter for defining the initiative, a set of incremental steps to define purpose, objective, desired results, stakeholders' steps, timelines, resources, and protocols for decision making and communications. This structure avoids lost time, lack of clarity, and tangential work. It provides focus in a common direction and mindset.

> *When working with a partner organization, a small technology company tracked sequential work with a project structure to ensure goals would be met. They were met and the joint efforts helped team members work together, grow, and acquire new skills from each other.*

Mode 14: Seeking New Opportunities

New opportunities come about in multiple and various ways. Being aware of all work outcomes and their implications is essential to uncovering these new opportunities. Reflection sessions on work outcomes, current events, and trends lead to new ideas and potential opportunities. Structures to support intrapreneurial thinking are available to support new opportunities. This thinking is recognized and rewarded routinely so that efforts to find new value are reinforced.

> *Holding global trend discussions led a human resources group to create a program for integrating immigrant populations into their small business initiatives as temporary contractors. They used a project approach to ensure that all understood the goal and work required to meet it. The immigrants and the businesses gained from this program, in revenue, stakeholdership, and new relationships.*

Integration and Alignment of Mindset Components

As extensively discussed through this chapter, mindset is made up of goals, values, beliefs, and mode of work. Once you can define each of these for yourself, it is important to contemplate how they support each other. Are your goals in line with your values? Do your beliefs align with your values? Does your mode of work reflect your goals, values, and beliefs? This alignment will strengthen your mindset with the self-confidence to actively pursue your destiny as a person and your legacy as a professional.

Once you are clear on these connections, your self-confidence in them will allow you to change them, as needed, to work with others or to accommodate a change or new opportunity.

Your self-determinism is wholly based on who you believe yourself to be. When you believe and continuously model the

> **Where do you find your mindset power?**

behaviors of that person, it is likely that others will believe your story, as well. Then you have the power to achieve.

Worksheet Reference

Worksheets to facilitate using the concepts in this chapter are found in "Developing the Intentional Mindset, Module 2: Understanding Mindset." The worksheets include:

Underlying Mindset of Autonomy: Goals, Values, Beliefs, Mode of Work

Aligning Behavioral Tendencies and Decisions to Mindset

Organizational Profile for Mindset, Individual Narrative, Network, and Growth

Stakeholder Profiles for Mindset, Narrative, Needs, Network, and Growth

Relevant Industry Mindsets

Community Mentality: Stories and Social Experiences

Chapter Summary

This chapter describes the components of a mindset and how to build awareness of them to manage them for best decision making. The next chapter describes the origins of these components for deep understanding of why and how they came to be.

CHAPTER 3

Origins of a Mindset

A small, privately owned execu-tive placement firm was founded by a man who studied behav-ioral economics in college. He was intrigued by the impact of the behaviors of those around

> **Mindset comes from some-place. You may not change the source, but you can change its impact.**

him. This background led him to add an innovative and unique ser-vice to his placement services of preparing people to understand and match the cultural, social, and operational mindsets of an organiza-tion before deciding to join. His insights helped his candidate clients and his organization clients fully understand and match their needs based on exploration of those mindsets and needs.

Pondering why you just behaved as you did? What sparked your emotion? Would another approach have been better? Is your thinking intuitive or shaped intentionally? The origins of mindset can be either, but are primarily based on a person's background or environment. When you understand the origin of an action, then it is possible to alter that think-ing to produce a better behavior, decision, and outcome. This would be considered a shift to an intentional mindset. So understanding your intuitive mindset, or your thinking, starts with exploring what causes a behavior or decision, in the context of actual outcomes.

Franklin Roosevelt (Goodwin 1994) recognized the necessity of learn-ing as essential to support his work as President of the United States before and during World War II. His challenge to learning was that he was crippled and couldn't travel. Franklin had to find other ave-nues to fulfill his need. He intuitively built multiple learning struc-tures in a most informal manner, beginning with his wife, Eleanor. Eleanor traveled to bring back the details of citizens' needs for

*Franklin to most effectively serve his Americans. He also held his cock-
tail hours daily to collect the thoughts and needs of his acquaintances.*

*Franklin and Eleanor often had conflicting priorities for achiev-
ing their goal of serving the country in difficult times. Eleanor made
the most brilliant contributions to the endeavor by understanding
the humanity of the American needs, while Franklin's efforts were
focused on sustaining democracy and security through his leadership
in managing world relationships. Eleanor was a master at integrating
Franklin's needs into her work of meeting the humanistic needs of the
country's people.*

*Franklin and Eleanor Roosevelt worked at their relationship
and altered it as circumstances dictated. They were married amid
significant resistance from Franklin's mother. As a possessive parent,
she was opposed to the marriage. However, Franklin and Eleanor
had a strong commitment to each other. After several years of marriage, Franklin breached that commitment with an extramarital
relationship that shocked Eleanor. Nonetheless, she saw her role as
extremely important in supporting her crippled husband who had
no use of his legs. Eleanor became Franklin's eyes and ears. They
developed an agreement on goals, values, and beliefs that facilitated their complementary work. They grew from their individual
and intuitive mindsets to a joint and intentional mindset for a
common goal.*

**Can you trace your mindset
to its origins? Do you understand how you might change
your mindset based on those
origins?**

When an outcome is negative,
consider what motivated your
behaviors and decisions. What
alternate behavior or decision
could have changed the outcome?
Was your goal not feasible? Was it
a value that you placed on some-
thing unrelated to the goal? Was it a belief, opinion, assumption, or bias
that led your behavior or decision to be shortsighted? Or was it your
mode of work that might have distorted your progress toward meeting
your desired outcome?

Assuming that you have identified your current mindset components,
knowing why you hold your current mindset, its origins, is significantly

helpful in changing them. For example, if you believe that only educated people can make valid decisions, you might want to explore why you think this. Was it your nature? Your nurture? An experience? When you know the source of that belief, then you can explore its validity and relevance to consider a change to that thinking.

The key ideas in this chapter include:

- Five sources to consider
- Nature and nurture
- Strengths
- Experiences
- Community mentality
- Uncertainties of our world

Five Sources to Consider

After building awareness of your mindset and connecting it to its origins, you may discover that a source is no longer relevant. This introspection can lead to modified thinking and better alignment of all of the mindset components to support each other for good decision making. There are five main sources of mindset to consider. They may overlap but it is easier to consider them separately so that an in-depth analysis is more feasible. They include:

- Nature and nurture
- Strengths
- Experiences
- Community mentality
- Uncertainties of our world

Learning, as a foundational value, is essential to understanding your mindset and the obstacles it may be presenting. Insights can come from all or any of these sources. When exploring your nature, nurture, and strengths, you may uncover unconscious characteristics of your mindset as they are established during your childhood years. When exploring experiences, community, and uncertainty, mindset is shaped as you live life throughout your growth and career. Exploring the uncertainties of your world is especially valuable as it sheds light on your current environment and, therefore, can help to align your mindset to the needs of current happenings and changes.

Considering all of these sources is most useful if you determine that a change is necessary in order to work more effectively toward an outcome. In most cultures, hurting others is not a positive force as part of your narrative. If you have a habit of hurting people because you value your own opinions too highly, then you might want to explore why you hold that value and how you might alter it to stop hurting people. Why do you hold that perspective of yourself? Reviewing and reflecting on your mindset very often sheds light on unconscious behaviors or decisions and related outcomes. Understanding the origins of how you think, behave, and decide allows you to consider changing or managing your mindset for better outcomes.

Learning about others' mindsets, as well as their origins, helps you to accommodate them for better outcomes when working together. Once identified along with their sources, reconciling mindsets includes several options. These include modifying your own mindset, helping another see the benefit of changing mindset, or abandoning the work because mindsets are too different and cannot be aligned.

Understanding others' mindsets also allows speculation on the value of those perspectives and how that value might influence your own mindset. Figure 3.1 describes the origins of mindset. Let's explore some details of the five sources.

Nature and Nurture	Strengths	Experiences	Community Mentality	Uncertainties
Birth, Parents	Hobbies	Jobs	Organization	Generational
Home location	Expertise	Mentors	Church, Religion	Exposure
Engagement	Levels of thinking	Network	Clubs	Current events
Learning style	Interests	Projects	Prof. associations	Development level
Rules and regs	Awards	Consequences	Family	Education
Behaviors	Goals	Opportunities		Opportunities
				Rewards
Values and Beliefs Risk tolerance, fear, uncertainty, entitlement, narrow-framing, overconfidence, lack of confidence, assertiveness, group well-being, power control, short- or long-term, individual or collective work				
Behaviors, Decisions, and Outcomes Link to beliefs and values				

Figure 3.1 Origins of a mindset

Nature and Nurture

The differentiation between nature and nurture structures is blurred. Psychologists have recently determined that current personalities are made up of 50 percent nature and 50 percent nurture, with the interaction of the two reinforcing and changing each other. When a person is born, a specific set of genetics defines the person. That person is usually nurtured by the holders of those genetics, so their nurturing will follow in that same vein, thus merging nature and nurture. They make up the foundational and natural traits that make up a person's temperament, personality, and foundational motivations for behaviors. These characteristics or traits stem from nature and, also, nurture. They include many considerations.

Eleanor Roosevelt (Goodwin 1994), wife of President Franklin Roosevelt, had a painful childhood. Her mother, a popular socialite, wanted a beautiful child to serve her own needs and often chided Eleanor for her lack of beauty and social skills. When her mother died at an early age, Eleanor was sent to live with her grandmother and then to a boarding school. Her father was supportive and loving as he doted on Eleanor. He was very special to her, but he was an alcoholic and died when Eleanor was ten years old. Her experience at the school was positive as she was very interested in learning about the world. It was a warm environment for her, as well. Unfortunately, her confidence was very low, stemming from her family interactions, and was only partially eased by the school experiences. This lack of confidence plagued her through her adult life and marriage. However, Eleanor had an exceptional sense of people's humanity and needs, probably due to her own upbringing. This perspective was extremely helpful to Franklin as he focused on legislation to serve those needs.

Franklin needed grass-roots knowledge of the people he served. His probing questions about what Eleanor saw in her travels and visits with these people helped her expand her initial observations. Franklin taught Eleanor how to investigate to uncover the information he needed to make relevant policies by asking questions that designed deeper and deeper levels of inquiry. She learned how to seek more clarity on relevant conditions of need and to explore to the point of fully understanding the causes of the needs. Therefore, she was able to identify what Franklin needed to know for policy decisions.

Eleanor and Franklin complemented each other, as he educated her in the art of investigation that served them both well. Eleanor's humanistic sensitivities complemented Franklin's intellect and strengths.

Common Cultural Value Dimensions

A culture study of IBM employees at global installations (Hofstede, Hofstede, and Minkov 2010) included 138 countries throughout the world. Hofstede interviewed these employees and identified six common values within their diverse cultures. He evaluated these value dimensions for importance within each country group, providing a guide for working with each country group. General descriptions include:

- **Power distance**—How far away from a decision are you comfortable?
- **Risk aversion**—How much risk can you tolerate?
- **Individualistic versus collectivistic work**—Do you like to work by yourself or within a group or team?
- **Feminine versus masculine approach**—Are you nurturing or more aggressive in your approach to work?
- **Time orientation**—Is time important to you when working?
- **Indulgence versus restraint**—Are you likely to indulge or restrain your investment in opportunities for growth and happiness?

How you personally value these dimensions gives insight into your mindset, as well as expectations of your behaviors and decisions. These value dimensions come from the nature and nurture of the environment within which you were born and raised. Natives of Finland have Finnish values and natives of France have French values, while Americans have their own values.

> **How did your birth environment and care takers shape your values?**

Invisible Capital

Your invisible capital (Raab 2010) is another aspect of your nature and nurture. Everyone has a unique set of background knowledge, values, interests, and connections. It includes everything

> **Are you aware of your invisible capital? How might its insights help you to build the narrative you desire?**

you know because you have been alive for so many years, including the multiple experiences that you have had. This invisible capital is extremely useful as a resource and network and is helpful in understanding your behaviors, their sources, and the ability to change them, as necessary. Also, recognizing your invisible capital as a resource can help you broaden and achieve your goals as you live your life.

> *Eleanor and Franklin formed a relationship based on their invisible capital. They knew each other as third cousins and were nurtured from the same social status and family perspective. This common background led to their understanding and love for each other, regardless of any unfortunate course of events in their lives.*

Perspectives acquired from nature and nurture can potentially facilitate behaviors and decisions needed for best outcomes. When understood, you can link these perspectives to achieving the desired outcomes of a project. Also, different perspectives can be used to circumvent an obstacle when navigating toward a goal. For example, if you, as an American, are trying to reach an agreement with a Chinese business colleague and difficulties have arisen, another Chinese colleague can be helpful in the conversation because he can present your idea from a Chinese perspective. Your Chinese friend and business colleague share a common nationality, or nurture, to facilitate understanding of your need. Agreement then happens because the two colleagues with similar mindsets have found a common path to agreement. Mindset is intuitively similar when it is rooted in a common nature or nurture.

Sometimes recognizing nature and nurture characteristics is enough to solve a mismatch with another as there are multiple ways

> **What are your characteristics of mindset that are grounded in nature or nurture?**

to find synergy for reaching a desired outcome. On occasion, you might opt to completely abandon a project when mindsets are just too far apart to reconcile. This choice is sometimes the best option for efficient use of resources.

Strengths

Recognizing and valuing your expertise and strengths allow you to make targeted growth goals. It is important to maximize what you are good at and intentionally build on it. It is more effective to focus on your areas of excellence as opposed to focusing on what you need to improve. This reinforces your strengths and helps you to value and maximize them for yourself and for your organization and/or community.

What do you enjoy doing? How do you like to help others? What do others recognize as your expertise? What do others ask you to do to help them? What do you do in your spare time? What do you do even when you are not paid to do it? Recognizing these areas as your strengths allows you to maximize them as you contribute to society. Working in these areas also boosts your self-confidence and this is most important to your autonomy. This approach to your strengths also, inadvertently, allows others to do the same with their strengths because you are not delving into their areas of expertise as a competitor. You are focused on your own domain and can build your narrative accordingly. Others can build their strengths in this same manner.

Being open to others' strengths gives insight and validity to their behaviors and decisions. How do you see others who do not share your strengths? Are their perspectives less valid? Or, perhaps, more valid due to their own recognized expertise? Do you view others' perspectives in the context of their strengths?

Recognizing these strengths in others can, also, help create a balance for working together. Doing what you are good at and letting others excel at what they are good at is often the most efficient and effective way to manage work and the ability to create new value. This approach also enhances your narrative as one who respects others and their excellence.

Your strengths shape your behaviors and decisions. When you are really good at something, you see an issue quite differently than someone with no expertise in that area. People who excel in an area may want to engage in related activities more than others who are not experts. This scenario can be thought of as an intuitive bias. It is not necessarily good or bad, but just important to be recognized for how it can impact the outcomes of work and working with others.

How do your strengths impact your goals, values, beliefs, and mode of work? What do you value because of your expertise? What do you disregard because of your expertise? These are questions that must always be asked. Would a behavior or decision be different if you were strong in other ways? Mindset perspectives are best understood in the context of your strengths.

Eleanor and Franklin had very different strengths. Eleanor was passionate about improving human conditions. She maximized that passion with projects that would add value to the current environment of the political world in which she and Franklin lived. She was persistent about her endeavors, using that passion to keep her work from falling short of her goals. She was content to slowly inch her progress along without completely abandoning her work due to the intense focus on a world at war.

Franklin could see that Eleanor's work on social needs and reform were important to enhance his political work and goals. His sequence of work was supported by his increasing understanding of Eleanor's passion and work for social reform. People were at the heart of both Franklin's and Eleanor's work.

Eleanor brought new perspectives on labor relations for Franklin to consider. The miners in Appalachia had dire needs that were unknown to outsiders or, seemingly, to politicians. The

> **What are the strengths that contribute to your mindset? What other strengths might be complementary to your strengths?**

miners' work and living brought them unnecessary pain and suffering. Eleanor's work was intense with her unrelenting focus to collect information for Franklin.

Experiences

People's mindsets, which lead to behaviors and decisions, are shaped by their experiences. Experiences teach unlimited lessons that shape your behaviors and decisions. Positive and negative outcomes of your work can often be linked to a specific experience. Getting to a true understanding of your experiences allows reflection on the mindset that fostered a behavior or decision. For example, many people feel disenfranchised by their experiences, leading to a lack of confidence. These experiences may be economic, family dysfunction, work-related, or socially-driven. Recognizing that these experiences have led to your lack of confidence allows you to explore that connection to validate it or not.

When an experience leaves you downtrodden and feeling excluded, you look for comfort. That comfort can be found with the realization that your behavior or decision may have caused the outcome. Exploring the source of that behavior or decision can help with validating it or not and therefore, create a new comfort with how to make an outcome better. When you speculate on a better outcome, you can then determine the better behavior or decision needed to arrive at that better outcome. This learning process builds confidence that you can be autonomous and in control of the outcomes of your work.

> **What makes you angry, sad, or isolated? What will alleviate these feelings for you?**

Experiences provide opportunities for your learning on a daily and continuous basis. Placing a value on learning helps you explore whatever seems curious. Exploring a situation's history and the stakeholders involved brings a new perspective to its cause. Why is someone frustrated with the self-service checkout technology in the supermarket? Does he believe that it is too complicated? Does he really want to talk to someone about his checkout? What experiences have set up his frustration? What does he need to eliminate the frustration?

Finally, experiences provide continuous context for reviewing and refreshing your mindset. Goals, values, beliefs, and mode of work change as the world changes. On any two days, events or experiences are never the same. A daily review of how a change might impact your mindset is not a luxury, but an essential part of keeping yourself current with the world around you. An autonomous person is routinely open to new learnings from new experiences.

> *During his political career, Joe Biden, President of the United States, (Rolnik and Shapira 2020) thought favorably of the DuPont Corporation as a conscientious corporation. It was a huge employer and philanthropic leader in his home state of Delaware. He considered it a corporation that practiced "stakeholder capitalism" as opposed to "shareholder capitalism." Biden later learned of a significant breach of stakeholder capitalism with new corporate leadership and the increased production and dumping of a toxic chemical with no regard for the populations it was impacting. Now he had to face the inconsistency of his previous positive impression with the current experience of the corporation's unethical behavior. His previous positive experiences gave him confidence that the previous leaders of the corporation could do better and fix the problem. His current experience of the treatment of the toxic chemical gave him doubt over the current leaders' intent. He had to balance these experiences to plan his next decisions to mitigate the risk that the new leaders presented.*

Hopefully, new experiences will foster some rethinking (Grant 2021). Tracking the changes in relevant areas and the experiences that come with the changes can prompt reconsiderations of your goals, values, beliefs, and mode of work. Calm reflections on unexpected outcomes can lead to insights into relevant behaviors and decisions, which can then lead to an evaluation of your mindset. Ultimately this practice keeps your mindset, behaviors, and decisions current to ensure your autonomy. If you are an expert letter writer but no one is communicating with letters due to electronic modes of connecting, you will want to reconsider how to use your strength differently in this new environment. Perhaps you will find a way to build the sensitive expression of your thoughts into the crispness and efficiency of "just in time" communication?

Consider how the change that happens in any one domain of your life impacts the other domains. Continuous reflection keeps you in control for assuring the destiny you seek. Change is not good or bad, it just is. Managing it for your own benefit is an exhilarating challenge.

> *Eleanor and Franklin had diverse interests but in order to work together and maintain their relationship, each had to compromise individual passions to accommodate the other. They had the same goal, which was to ensure the well-being of the American people. Their individual experiences led them to different paths to this goal. They understood that about each other and worked together to integrate their work, Franklin on the security front and Eleanor on the social front. They used their passions to contribute to each other's progress toward the common goal. They were able to see the commonality in these pursuits. Having a strong democracy is the support infrastructure needed to serve security, social, and humanitarian needs.*

What experience has changed your mindset recently?

Community Mentality

When people belong to or join a group, such as an organization, an association, or a profession, there are expected and respected mindsets in place. Engineers are focused on precision, artists are focused on creativity and openness, and social scientists are interested in the human condition. Members firmly value, believe, and act on these behavioral expectations (Haidt 2012). Members will agree or disagree with an external and opposing view based on these expectations and mindset. Change from this expected mindset is much too difficult for people to consider. People tend to adhere to their original value and belief in their modes of thinking, acting, and deciding. What happens when this mindset doesn't change with a change in the environment?

> *The behavioral rituals that define a group of insurgents, such as the Taliban (Gill 2021), give them strength of conviction and commitment to collective action. Especially religious groups with strict behavioral guidelines create this commitment to community action.*

"Religious organizations are 'club goods,' wherein members share collective benefits, such as welfare provision and fellowship. These benefits depend on active contribution. If everyone participates willingly, the organization is vibrant."

There is a very distinct allegiance to the community to which you belong (Akerlof and Kranton 2011). There are expected and necessary behaviors for industries, expertise of professional groups, organizations, and customers. Police officers will value physical safety while teachers will value student engagement and state legislators will value high test scores. Doctors will value medical treatments while patients may value "wait and see" approaches, comparing the side effects of medication versus the symptoms of a diagnosed condition. These mindsets must be considered when working with someone outside of your own area of community.

There are religious, nationality, professional, and community beliefs. What would make you change any of these beliefs? Perhaps some experiences that counter these beliefs? Or some data or information that change the nature of your beliefs and resulting outcomes? When, why, and is abortion OK? How about capital punishment? Might an experience change your belief?

> **Do your opinions and actions align with your values?**

Most surprisingly, people pursue an interest in or support a rising star based on others' actions (Brooks 2022). The Beatles music became popular because people followed their friends' interests. Fortunately for the Beatles, a following and their subsequent fame was due to a contagious interest. Community think is very powerful. People follow what their friends follow. Awareness of this trend might suggest reconsidering your own personal preferences. Consider whether a popular belief aligns to your own goals, values, and mode of work?

Eleanor's eagerness to learn was part of a new mindset to establish her individual value to Franklin and to her country. Eleanor had to reconsider her nature and nurture and its values to make herself of use to her country and to her husband. She observed, questioned, and requestioned her fellow Americans to obtain invaluable insights for Franklin and his pursuits. Eleanor and Franklin learned together to design an approach to fulfill their joint goal of service to the American people.

Eleanor was phenomenal as she built her mindset of autonomy with absolutely no authority. She had the urge to be useful and knew the strengths she had to contrib-

> **What are your community mentalities?**

ute for the social welfare of her country. She made her own path to leadership and engagement in the social community wherever and whenever she saw the slightest opportunity, such as joining the Red Cross in Europe to help distribute needed goods to soldiers and citizens. Her interest, motivation, and skills were apparent to everyone who watched her work. She became a hero of the people and, consequently, an asset to Franklin.

Uncertainties of Our World

World events, local events or conflicts, general economic conditions, and personal/emotional scenarios always impact behaviors and decisions. Understanding these current concerns regarding yourself or a stakeholder helps to identify mindsets that are driving diverse behaviors and decisions.

The New York Stock Exchange is impacted by the uncertainty of events and conditions, interest rates, and market activity. Stock valuations go up and down not on any concrete basis, but on the daily observations of activity and people's mindsets concerning them. When your activity is based on uncertainty, you might behave and make decisions that attempt to mitigate that uncertainty. Oil prices, which impact most global citizens directly and indirectly, are a catalyst for fluctuating evaluations. This is not necessarily connected to any concrete outcome, but does create worry that it might enormously impact your life. When people are uncertain, they can be most unpredictable in their behaviors and decisions. They may act based on worst case scenarios, depending on where they fall on Hofstede's value dimensions and approaches to work. Making a connection between behaviors and intent helps to identify supporting mindsets, which can give direction on how these mindsets may need modification for better outcomes.

Although Franklin Roosevelt's mode of work often seemed chaotic and disorderly, his plan was for that scenario to prompt many conflicting opinions and perspectives. By working in less than a structured manner, he was able to listen for nuggets of value to be combined with other nuggets for greater value. Make no mistake, he was in charge of the chaos for his own reasons as he rationalized it with its contribution to effective decision making. His goal and value was on building trust and relationships to gain insights into complex conditions. The unstructured approach allowed for candid opinions and biases to be shared. He got his clues on how best to proceed from these unstructured experiences.

Both Roosevelts focused on the process more than the result as they understood that a better result would come out of the process of their work. Convincing stakeholders in Congress of the need to prepare to mobilize a strong military required an intentional process of communication that was implemented through his seemingly unstructured leadership. Trust was established and change was accepted.

Economic conditions that may be perceived as uncertain might include inflation, salary restrictions, job loss, pandemics, housing difficulties, and food costs and availability.

Emotional conditions that may be perceived as uncertain might include family difficulties, child care obstacles, divorce or separation, education availability, and family responsibilities.

Success and Luck (Frank 2016) discusses the importance of luck in your life. Often an advantage just comes with your birth, connections, or experiences. This would be due to luck. Since luck is not assured, it adds to the uncertainties in life. However, you can intentionally create a lucky environment to support your efforts. Aligning yourself to the right work conditions, opportunities, or an area of passion will undoubtedly provide you with some luck in reaching your goals.

These uncertain conditions can very clearly impact your goals, value, beliefs, and mode of work. Attention will most likely be on short-term needs before longer-term needs.

Sometimes Eleanor's intense mode of work was too much for Franklin, especially during war time when he needed to unwind and relax to be able to manage the stress of the international arena of World War II. Franklin and Eleanor at this point had to accommodate each other's needs. Franklin worked with Missy, his assistant, to create those relaxing times through the cocktail hours and visits with guests. He made a practice of continually learning from others as he invited various and diverse guests into his routine and daily cocktail hour.

Eleanor felt left out of this arrangement but found comfort on her own as countrymen always greeted her with great acclaim and appreciation for her efforts. She was extremely popular. This acclaim satisfied her and motivated her to continue her work.

These two arrangements allowed them to continue their complementary work while seeking satisfaction individually through separate activities in addition to their collaboration that they made sure to continue.

Franklin believed that the United States needed to build out its military after World War I, even though the general consensus of the Congress and the American people was to minimize military forces and investment because we would never enter another war. Franklin saw a bigger picture and knew that we had to support our allies to protect the democracy that the Americans and Europeans had so painfully won. He tempered his thoughts and speeches to comfort and allow people to evolve to his way of thinking. He would not give up his campaign to support and strengthen democracy in America and as a world priority. Eleanor was viewed throughout the country as the human side of Franklin's endeavors.

What uncertainties impact your mindset?

According the Psychologist Viktor Frankl (Perel 2021), "Everything can be taken from a man but one thing: the last of the human freedoms—to choose one's attitude in any given set of circumstances." Circumstances are more often than not uncertain.

Worksheet Reference

Worksheets to facilitate using the concepts in this chapter are found in Developing the Intentional Mindset, Module 2: Understanding Mindset. The worksheets include:

Underlying Mindset of Autonomy: Goals, Values, Beliefs, Mode of Work

Aligning Behavioral Tendencies and Decisions to Mindset

Organizational Profile for Mindset, Individual Narrative, Network, and Growth

Stakeholder Profiles for Mindset, Narrative, Needs, Network, and Growth

Relevant Industry Mindsets

Community Mentality: Stories and Social Experiences

Chapter Summary

This chapter describes the origins of your mindset components, which helps to understand why you think the way you do. The next chapter provides examples of various behaviors and decisions and how you might analyze each for best understanding.

CHAPTER 4

Behavioral Concepts and Examples

A brilliant accounting student accepted a position with a very large and highly prestigious professional services firm upon graduation. She was full of a desire

> **Observing and analyzing others' behaviors and decisions are essential for autonomy.**

to learn and grow in her new position, as she had been trained to intrapreneur and was looking forward to these challenges. She worked for two years before she determined that the strict culture, processes, and protocols of the firm were not going to allow her to grow as she wished. None of her colleagues were thinking about new value as an intrapreneur. They could only focus on meeting the demands of their daily work. She was not a match for this firm and took her leave to find a new opportunity in which she could design her own learning and progress.

What went wrong with that conversation you just had? Why did your long-time friend stop calling you? What did you say that made an adversary into your friend?

Mindsets are powerful. Thought patterns and connections are unique to each individual. To capitalize on these differences and not be derailed by them, it is best to get out in front of them and understand them before they negatively impact you or your destiny. The behaviors and decisions that result from your mindset are predictable if you are aware of that mindset. Detecting the connection is often a challenge, but not impossible. Connections are subtle but can be identified with insight into your background and experiences. Others' mindsets may also be integrated into the behaviors, decisions, and results you are exploring.

Can you link a recent behavior or decision to an outcome? Would you change that behavior or decision if you could?

This chapter provides some sample behavioral concepts, outcomes, and possible mindset causes. Often observing these behaviors in others helps you to identify them within your own behaviors and decisions. If you are honest and realistic about the rationale behind each of these behaviors and decisions, you have a chance at testing the validity of the mindset cause and changing it to make better outcomes, if needed, next time. The impact of mindset of your behaviors and decisions is huge. Don't discount why you do what you do. Explore when things go right and when they go wrong, the mindset cause, and the source of that mindset. Consider the same for others to explore the rationale behind their behaviors and decisions, as well. You will find clues to better outcomes.

The sample mindsets that are presented here are based on the goals, values, beliefs, and mode of work that are described in Chapter 2 "Defining Mindset Components." Keep in mind that these mindsets have their sources in five areas as described in Chapter 3 "Origins of a Mindset." They include:

1. **Nature and nurture**—being born and raised
2. **Strengths**—what you are naturally interested in and good at
3. **Experiences**—what you encounter and how it impacts you
4. **Community mentality**—the common thinking of your groups
5. **Uncertainties of our world**—changes, future and real time, that may impact you

Mindsets may also be attributed to a combination of these sources. For example, experiences may depend on your community mentality and your nurtured past. Be open in your considerations of sources so that your mindset can be fully understood and managed. You will, most likely, find some surprises in your realizations.

Gertrude Bell (Howell 2006) and Abraham Lincoln (Goodwin 2006) have distinct backgrounds that created their mindsets. Consider their unique values, challenges, and their sources.

Gertrude Bell started life with family trust and relationship that sustained her throughout her life. Her adventuresome goals of exploration of the middle east were unique to her times but she maintained the support of her family of stakeholders who believed in her capabilities, talents, and quest for adventure. Her autonomous mindset allowed her to build the trust of those from foreign cultures in order to help them achieve their goals of self-determinism. She was never daunted by uncertainties or intimidated by danger. Her confidence was unrelenting.

Lincoln (Goodwin 2006) was an observer of people and their mindsets. His concept of democracy led him to believe that men should be entitled to the rewards of what they produce. As a young man, Lincoln's father sent him to work for a neighbor and then kept the wages for himself. Perhaps Lincoln's bias in the direction of freedom, providing the circumstances and environment needed for people to be free to earn and shape their own lives, was due to his experience as a young man. This was a bias that was not held by all politicians of his time. Every man interpreted the country's constitution according to his individual perspective of freedom and equality.

> **Can you link a behavior and decision to your mindset and its source?**

The key ideas in this chapter include:

- Potential behaviors and mindsets
- Outcomes of those behaviors
- Mindsets that caused those behaviors

Potential Behaviors and Mindsets

Much has been written about the mindfulness that can sustain people in a complex world. If you can diagnose outcomes in the context of your mindset, it is very possible to change those outcomes. Being aware and managing your mindset for good outcomes makes sense. Included here is a selection of some meaningful behavioral concepts as context for your analysis of your own mindset and its connections to your outcomes. Also, understanding others' mindsets can give you invaluable clues as to how to most effectively work with them. The following behavioral concepts should give helpful perspectives on how and why we all work and make decisions.

Corporate Mindsets

Consider five corporate mindsets and the environments that create them (Kennedy and Deal 2000). They are helpful for understanding stakeholder mindsets and how you might manage them. Table 4.1 describes corporate mindsets.

Table 4.1 Corporate mindsets

Mindsets and Descriptions	Environments That Create These Mindsets
Tough-guy, macho—High risk, aggressive, individual stars, no cooperation, quick feedback, cohesion difficult, low value on long term	• Marketing • Police • Surgeons • TV • Advertising • Sports
Work hard/play hard—Small risk, hyperactive, quick/intensive feedback, short term, persistence, benign	• Sales • Manufacturing • Real estate • Door-to-door sales • Computer companies
Bet-Your-Company—High risk, slow feedback, focus on future, long-term ambiguity, hierarchy, respect for authority, persistent pressure, long-term trivial work	• R&D • Oil companies • Boeing • NASA • Mining • Investment banks • Army/Navy
Process—Low risk, slow or no feedback, focus on how, bureaucracy, protectiveness and caution, system integrity versus individual roles, enables other cultures	• Accounting • Banks • Insurance companies • Financial services • Utilities • Pharma

Most people probably fall in-between some of these categories but they give a starting point for identifying narratives and mindsets of stakeholders. Identifying the mindset of a stakeholder allows you to meet those needs to build trust and relationship.

> **Do you consider your stakeholders' mindsets when you disagree with them?**

Example and outcome: Bankers and insurance companies have strict guidelines for the implementation of their services. When deviations are requested, they will return to the rule book for decisions. Exceptions to these rules are hard to justify and your issue may not be accommodated to your satisfaction.

Mindset causes might include the community mentality of the group and subsequent environment.

Marketing Strategies

Analyzing buyers before designing a marketing strategy makes the marketing campaign much more relevant and effective (Rapaille 2006). If you know the mindset of a potential buyer or market, messages and products can be designed to build trust, relationship, and stakeholdership with these buyers to increase or ensure sales.

> **What mindset characteristics will engage clients to work with you alone?**

Example and outcome: Think Company attracts clients with the thought that they want to enhance the lives of their customers and employees (and, therefore, the success of the business). Thinkers use this goal to convince clients that they can work only with Think Company due to their highly customized approach and results. Think Company strives to retain clients to serve their future needs and most often retains clients with this understanding.

Mindset cause might include a value on satisfying and engaging stakeholders based on their specific needs and a goal of continuing that service in the future.

Behavioral Tendencies

Behavioral tendencies (Ariely 2009) describe potential emotional responses based on values and beliefs. Exploring why you or a colleague demonstrate a behavioral tendency can lead to the enabling value or belief, and then the possibility of changing it for a better outcome. They include:

- **Fear of an outcome**—belief in a potential negative outcome
  Example and outcome: An executive's assistant failed to pass on a message to his boss due to fear of being held responsible for bad news. Lack of communication results in his boss not addressing a problem and being chastised for perceived lack of interest.

  Mindset causes might include a lack of strength, self-confidence, or an uncertainty of a boss' behaviors.

- **Entitlement to something not earned**—belief that one is owed something due to a connection or relationship
  Example and outcome: A new graduate thought she would automatically be given a position at her father's company. Her lack of preparation for the interview or the position didn't earn her the position as competitors were many.

  Mindset cause might include the family community mentality that striving to earn is not important if you are a member of the family. Natural consequences of minimal preparation have not been allowed to occur.

- **Overconfidence for achieving a result**—belief in self with no background or experience to support that confidence
  Example and outcome: A university student worked at a financial services company for a summer and decided she did not need to study for an upcoming financial examination due to her experience. She failed the examination and had to retake it for a required certification.

  Mindset cause might include her experiences when she was successful without any preparation in areas of her intuitive strengths, not in an area that required new learning.

- **Risk aversion of a loss or difficulty**—belief that risk of a potential loss or obstacle is too high
  Example and outcome: A junior law associate has decided not to take a challenging promotion because of the risk of failure, even though the learning gained from the promotion would

propel her to more promotions. Learning in the new and challenging work domain was lost and she was labeled as a noninterested employee.

Mindset cause might be a family belief that only success matters, not learning.

- **Narrow framing of a problem**—belief that the very short-term context of a problem is definitive
Example and outcome: When faced with an immediate shortage of a production essential, a young manager bought a smaller quantity of a needed product for a low price but at a higher unit price. The manager overspent for this product and put his budget balance at risk for future purchases. His budget only allowed for the lower bulk price of the essential component.

Mindset cause might be a belief that short-term action is expeditious and most effective as opposed to taking a longer-term view of the total supply needed.

- **Loss aversion versus appreciation of a gain**—belief that loss is more significant than gain, even if the amount is the same
Example and outcome: When playing poker for money, a young man felt that a $10 loss is far more significant than a $10 win. He was worried about a loss to the point of compromising his potential to win with a far too conservative approach.

Mindset cause might include an uncertainty of available resources to support his poker efforts.

- **Confirmation**—looking for validation of what a person already thinks
Example and outcome: From 2000 to 2005, many hopeful home buyers assumed large mortgages to buy their dream homes. The banks told them that they would be able to make the payments, even when the payments escalated due to adjustable mortgage rates. By 2006, many home buyers had defaulted on their mortgages, causing a drop in home prices due to the defaults. The health of the economy was impacted, as well.

Mindset cause might include a community mentality that everyone is entitled to home ownership, the American dream.

- **Desirability**—looking for accommodation of a person's desires
Example and outcome: Some U.S. citizens in 2020 believed that the presidential election was invalid due to voting fraud, even though multiple investigations showed no evidence of any fraud. Division in the country paralyzed Congress and many other state legislators in their ability to legislate for their constituents.

Mindset cause might include a community fear of their political party losing control socially, economically, and culturally.

- **Heuristics**—relying on status quo conditions to make decisions
Example and outcome: In acquiring a company, the owner of the acquiring company assumed that their current culture would be agreeable to the newly acquired company members. No considerations or accommodations of the acquired company culture were explored. The company to be acquired pulled out of the deal at the last minute as they were not satisfied with the integration of their employees into the acquiring company's current organizational structure.

> **What are your behavioral tendencies and what are their origins? Are these tendencies valid today?**

Mindset cause was probably a belief that the acquiring organization was most desirable and others would be happy to join as dictated by the acquirer.

Neural Mirror

A neural mirror (Goleman 2005) refers to an emotional response returned to a messenger that mirrors the emotion of the messenger. A smile evokes a smile. Confusion evokes concern. But what do these messages mean to the efforts to trust, build relationship, and collaborate?

How do you present yourself to others? Are you always affirmative even when you do not agree with someone's perspective? What message are you giving through your inadvertent smile, frown, confusion, or curiosity? Meaning is taken from your unspoken message. How might this behavior impact a decision, either your own or that of a stakeholder? Do you regard the response to your smile or frown as agreement to the message that you just sent?

Uncovering a neural mirror in a response can help you clarify a truer response, feeling, or mindset so that outcomes are not negatively impacted by a divergent mindset.

Example and outcome: Babies will smile back at you almost inevitably. What do they mean by that smile? They are communicating their comfort, engagement, and are relating to an external world.

Mindset cause might include an adult's value on engaging and comforting a child, or a need for approval from the child.

> **When have you used a neural mirror and what was the result?**

Conservative and Liberal Brains

Physical brain structures can cause your thinking to be conservative or liberal (Denworth 2020). Liberalism has been associated with the gray matter volume of the anterior cingulate cortex. Conservatism has been associated with an increased size of the right amygdala. These structures offer possible rationales for cognitive styles of liberals and conservatives. Understanding another's cognitive style in this context helps describe the mindset behind an unexpected or divergent decision.

> **What is your conservative or liberal tendency and is it similar to your genetic background (your parents)?**

Example and outcome: Politicians, who believe so vehemently in their perspectives and causes, may not be physically able to fathom another perspective. Agreement with a diverse view is not possible.

Mindset causes might include nature as physical attributes of brain structures are determined genetically at birth.

Co-Intrapreneuring

Co-intrapreneuring is a learned practice that enables workers together to take control and be responsible for innovative thinking (Wunderer 2001).

Including this practice in an organizational narrative will encourage intra-preneuring and the pursuit of new value. It includes the following beliefs and behaviors:

- **Meaning through vision**—using the context of vision to make meaningful connections
- **Change as an opportunity**—openness to leveraging change for improvement
- **Willingness to make mistakes and learn**—flexibility to use trial and error in order to learn
- **Committed support of ideas**—continuous inquiry into new avenues for creating value
- **Continuous improvement**—awareness of the continuous need to strive for improvement
- **Long-term cooperative orientation**—recognizing the need for the dependence of autonomy
- **Mutual trust and freedom**—using stakeholdership for building autonomy
- **Customer-orientation**—recognizing the customer as a stakeholder

Example and outcome: Baird of Philly Foodworks made a co-intra-preneuring environment possible and credible with his approach of fostering coresponsibility for decision making. This environment resulted in large-scale managed growth for the company.

Mindset causes might include a value in a community mentality to engage and maximize the diverse perspectives of the members of the growing community.

Theory X, Y, Z

Beliefs, opinions, and assumptions about what motivates people to work and how they work are described by three management theories (MacGregor 2006; Ouchi 1981). Theory X holds that people need specific direction to guide work at all times. Theory Y holds that people are self-motivated and enjoy the challenge of defining their own work, goals, and successes in the context of organizational goals. Theory Z, called "Japanese Management" style holds that high productivity is based on employee morale, motivation, satisfaction, and subsequent growth. Awareness and use of these theories help leaders define the work environment necessary for best productivity and performance.

Example and outcome: Think Company's CEO believes in the power of a vision and strives to establish a common vision for both Thinkers and clients. He combines Theory Y and Theory Z in his approach to defining work. Clients are very satisfied as Think Company solutions are relevant and tailored to their unique needs.

> **Do you prefer to work based on theory X, theory Y, theory Z, or a combination of these environments? Why do you prefer that environment?**

Mindset cause might include a belief in people's ability to take control of their destinies and that of their stakeholders to do the same, simultaneously.

Giver, Taker, Matcher

Consider three reciprocity styles of behavior, which are givers, takers, and matchers (Grant 2014), and their impact to your success. Givers are most interested in helping others. Takers are most interested in their own interests. Matchers are interested in matching others' gains with their own gains. Behaviors label people into one of these three categories and seem to determine their success in life.

Givers are often not considered successful early on in their endeavors because they are too busy accommodating others' needs. But in longer-term context, their giving nature endows them with invisible capital that is so supportive that they are the most successful in the end. Takers and matchers are more successful early in their endeavors but fall far behind givers in the long run.

Using these labels can help you identify, mitigate, and manage these behaviors for individuals' and organizational benefit. When people gain insights into the outcomes of their behaviors, they are more likely to manage them effectively.

Example and outcome: Gertrude Bell was a giver who eventually benefitted from her unending behaviors and decisions to give without need for return. Her unrelenting efforts earned her great respect and acclaim as an international hero.

> **Are you a giver? Taker? Matcher? Have you benefitted from any of these approaches?**

Mindset cause might include a nurtured sense of her value and her strength to explore the unknown.

Flow Thinking for Highest and Most Efficient Achievement

Optimal experiences happen when one reaches a genuinely satisfying state of consciousness, called *flow*. During *flow*, people typically experience deep enjoyment, creativity, and a total involvement with life and/or a pursuit (Csikszentmihalyi 2008). This psychological description demonstrates the ways this positive state can be pursued and achieved, not just left to chance. By ordering the information that enters your consciousness to create a state of *flow*, you can discover true happiness, unlock your potential, and greatly improve the quality of your life and work.

Example and outcome: Alexander Hamilton (Chernow 2004) entered this state of flow as a young orphan. He continuously sought ways to create value for others as he built a future for himself. He used his natural writing and ideation skills to support George Washington during the revolutionary war. He was unrelenting in his flow of activity and undeterred by enemies or obstacles. He made extremely significant and recognized contributions to the infrastructure of the new country.

> **What triggers your state of *flow*? How do you engage those triggers for support?**

Mindset causes might include his strengths in writing and thinking and his intentional management of the uncertainty that enveloped his young life.

Five Stages of Development

Abraham Maslow defined five levels of development that enable and guide actions and decisions toward your goals (Smith 2017). This framing can be applied to human development or to the goals of a specific initiative. The stages are sequential and must be achieved in the order presented. Table 4.2 describes these stages of development.

Table 4.2 Maslow's stages of development

Stage 1: Physiological needs—seeking satisfaction of physical needs, such as food and water
Stage 2: Security needs—seeking satisfaction of safety needs, security of a home with heat and comfort
Stage 3: Belonging needs—seeking a sense of belonging to a group, a team, or community
Stage 4: Esteem—seeking respect or recognition as a person, a professional, or contributor
Stage 5: Self-actualization—seeking the ability to create new value with innovation

If you are not secure in your position within a new organization, you will not be able to ultimately pursue an innovation. If a child is hungry when arriving at school, it is impossible for that child to trust and relate with other students or the teacher until his hunger is routinely satisfied. Understanding your current stage of development when initiating a project will help you pursue relevant work to progress to self-actualize in this domain.

Example and outcome: A newly founded software company decided to acquire another company to expand its products. Since the acquiring company was not entirely comfortable with its own departmental and operational flow, they couldn't achieve the self-actualization of expanding the company. The acquisition was chaotic, cost more than was necessary, and was not successful in expanding the products of the combined companies.

Mindset causes might include the lack of nurturing, leadership development, and overconfidence in the ability to succeed in acquiring the other company.

> **What is your level of development related to a recent project?**

Delusional Thinking

A mindset often seeks confirmation of an already held value or belief (Vedantam and Mesler 2021). The delusional belief directs actions and decisions to validate and support your delusion. Selective and biased research helps you to confirms these beliefs. What you want to believe rings true based on delusional thinking and biased research. Listening to others' perspectives on a topic can help you identify your delusions. Seeing the bias in your research will also lead to more realistic perspectives. Identifying your delusions will bring reality to your work and outcomes to be achieved.

Example and outcome: Executives often believe that all is well in their organizations because they want all to be well. Denying or ignoring telltale signs of inefficiency, missed goals, lack of satisfaction and motivation, and retention among customers and employees leads to further dysfunction and loss.

> **What beliefs do you hold that confirm your wishes?**

Mindset cause might include uncertainty of value and strength in a specific domain. This uncertainty could be caused by childhood crises and less assured care taking.

Research Biases

While asking the right questions, the right research also is important. Often your current values and beliefs can limit the questions and research you conduct. Biases can be implicit and beyond your awareness. They can limit the possibilities that you may consider in your research. For example, if you believe that electric cars are not going to last into the future, you will discredit and not consider any research that refers to longer-term use and value of electric cars. Limiting your questions and research because of your beliefs can eliminate essential insights for improving outcomes or new opportunities. Seeking others' opinions of your research findings can help you question your beliefs and their alignment to your goals and values. Perhaps your values and goals are not aligned either?

Example and outcome: Think Company Thinkers strive to determine the real goals and values of a company before they start working on the stated goal and value to be created. With clarity and agreement of all workers on the goal, research and work meet desired results, as intended.

> **What are your assumptions that designed your research on a recent project?**

Mindset cause might include a mode of work that is not limited by time, thus allowing the depth of research needed for clarity and goal agreement.

Scout Versus Soldier

Personas can identify people as scouts or soldiers (Julia Galef 2021). Scouts lead and map the course of activity for others. Soldiers take their lead from scouts. Scouts are leaders and soldiers are followers. When people are identified as either, there can be some conclusions drawn about their mindsets, including values and beliefs. What mindset frame are you applying to structure your work? Expecting a soldier to scout will most likely not work. Considering your behavior on a recent project will help you identify as a scout or a soldier. What do you need to be in a specific situation?

Example and outcome: Alexander Hamilton was a scout in all of his experiences. He constantly looked for opportunities to serve others in a way that would create some value and develop his own expertise. He was recognized as a major force in the development of the new democracy.

Mindset cause might include Hamilton's need to use his strengths to lead to opportunity for himself and his stakeholders, with whom he shared a value in democracy.

> **When do you behave as a scout? When do you behave as a soldier? Are they intentional choices?**

Satisfaction and Motivation

Herzberg's motivation and satisfaction theories add great clarity to workers' happiness (Nickerson 2023). People are satisfied by compensation, company policy, and relationship with a supervisor. People are motivated by growth opportunities, recognition, responsibility, achievement, and advancement. Satisfaction and motivation are different from each other. Leaders can impact the behaviors of workers by tending to both satisfaction and motivation factors in creating an environment for autonomy. Surveying or observing workers' satisfaction and motivation levels can keep leaders current on workers' needs, retaining them and their value for the organization.

Example and outcome: Corporate executives who try to retain employees with high compensation are discounting the need for motivational dimensions in employees' experiences. Satisfaction doesn't presume retention because people need motivation to be engaged in a common initiative to encourage them to stay.

> **What motivates you? What satisfies you? What makes you most productive, satisfaction or motivation?**

Mindset cause might include executives' belief that money is the most important motivator due to their own nurtured value structure or experience with too little compensation.

Thinking and Rethinking

People make rash and quick status quo decisions that do not serve them well (Grant 2021). Reconsidering a quick thought with possible outcomes is a good use of your energy. These outcomes provide a new level of insight into your initial thought. If you always respond to a crisis as done before, a status quo decision could end in disaster. Behaviors and decisions are best when they are advised by a second thought. How is this situation different or the same? Working in the accelerated 21st century challenges workers to rethink decisions. Building time into a schedule for rethinking is essential in support of good decision making.

Example and outcome: Eleanor and Franklin balanced each other by thinking and rethinking together. Due to their differing perspectives, they helped each other in arriving at plans and approaches to satisfy various citizens' needs.

> **What triggers you to rethink a behavior or decision? Do you collaborate on ideas and actions?**

Mindset cause might include their common nurturing that valued service to others. Eleanor and Franklin also created great strength together as they worked toward a common goal but from differing perspectives that could encompass all needs.

Communication Styles

Grant identifies four communication/discussion styles that carry unique messages to the listener. These messages may not be your intended message, so rethinking them to adjust the message to your intended message is helpful. Awareness of the reality and impact of your communication is insightful. The four message styles include:

- **Preacher**—Do you instruct people in what they should think or do? Are you sending the unintended message that people do not know what to think or do?
- **Prosecutor**—Do you accuse people of their shortcomings? Are you intending to reduce a person's self-confidence so that they get stuck in their thinking?
- **Political**—Do you advise people with the context of a political perspective? Do you intend to devalue a person's current thinking as the wrong way to think?
- **Scientific inquiry**—Do you seek to understand the science behind a dilemma? Do you use an inquiry approach so that you set up a joint thinking initiative to arrive at a common and rethought consensus?

Building your own and others' awareness of how communication is received helps you refine your communication style to different situations. Explaining your style and its purpose is helpful to give context to listeners and for more probable alignment to the message.

Example and outcome: Derek Jeter takes charge of his baseball playing efforts with an inquiry into the most helpful scoring for each situation. He is not worrying about preaching, prosecuting, or politicizing his energy for his own achievement. This approach has resulted in wide acclaim and recognition for being a strong player and winner.

Mindset cause might include a value on team achievement, as opposed to his own achievement.

> **How do you approach interactions with others? Do you consider mindsets in choosing a relevant mode for each interaction?**

Chapter Summary

This chapter presents sample behaviors and decisions and the rationale for them. The next chapter describes how you can create your own goals and values, as well as align them with each other.

Building an Autonomous Mindset

CHAPTER 5

Your Goals and Values

A small software company decided to acquire a competitor to increase product offerings. The acquiring company had a goal of integrating this company into its current organization, assuming that their own goals and val-

> **Goals and values comple- ment each other and set the platform for beliefs, mode of work, and your resulting nar- rative.**

ues were aligned. The acquiring company's goal was to control and increase its market share. The company values included collaborative efforts. Control and collaboration did not align. The mismatch of the acquirer's own goals and values was troblesome to the owner of the company to be acquired. The acquisition did not happen. There was a significant waste of resources and time on this initiative.

Do you think about every action or decision in terms of its outcome toward your goal? Do outcomes sometimes come as a surprise? Might your actions be sparked by an unconscious value that you hold? Think- ing about the outcome of every effort before it is undertaken provides a guide for achieving an expected outcome. It also provides context for what you actually value.

Mindset leads to your decisions, and your decisions lead to your des- tiny and/or legacy. Setting goals and values is the first step in shaping your mindset. Where you are going, what you want to achieve, and what values will support that quest are determined through your goals and values. Your strengths, interests, activities, and knowledge give you a start to shaping your goals. You create your narrative with your work toward your goals. Make your goals meaningful to the narrative you would like to create.

These goals create a path for you. They can be reviewed and changed when conditions change, but it is better to change a goal than to have no direction. Goals can drive daily activity as they guide that activity toward a milestone or a time deadline. Envision what the result of this work should look like when it is complete. Are you attempting to learn something, win something, meet a deadline, or some of each? In all cases, the incremental goals should be contributing to and aligned with your vision and mission.

A mindful presence that comes with the focus of a goal gives you extra energy to persist in the right direction. It makes work a meaningful experience that doesn't feel like drudgery.

Being totally immersed in your work is a condition that facilitates a presence of mind (Csikszentmihalyi 2008). Csikszentmihalyi describes the state of mind that facilitates complete focus and attention to the task at hand. It is a very deliberate focus, called *flow*, that yields superb results and outcomes. This complete focus is on the goal to be achieved.

This chapter explores the importance of understanding and making goals and values that will lay the foundation for your desired narrative, ensuring that they are complementary to each other, and matching them to the goals and values of your organization and stakeholders. These are the three most significant aspects of your mindset for ensuring success in your efforts.

The key ideas in this chapter include:

- Understanding and making goals and values
- Defining your desired narrative
- Defining and aligning to organizational and stakeholder goals and values

Understanding and Making Goals and Values

Why are goals and values so important? They assure that you will be working on something that is meaningful to you. They give you direction and purpose. Research shows that motivation in life is much more meaningful than the satisfaction of salary and a pleasant environment. Setting goals and working toward them are necessary to put you on a track for highest motivation. What are you striving for? What will make you happy? Knowing what you want is the first step to achieving that happiness.

Values include the core principles by which you live your life. A core value might be honesty or selflessness or happiness or learning or helping others. The list of values is endless and depends only on what you treasure most in living your life. Knowing what core principles you stand for can give helpful direction when faced with a dilemma around a decision. Values guide you in working toward your ambitions and goals.

Goals and values give context and direction. When uncertainty is all around you, a solid direction answers the question of what to do next. Company leaders use goals and values to focus workers in a common direction. One company values customer satisfaction. All dilemmas are solved with this value in mind since the customer is always to be accommodated. Another leader values highest quality as the company's main strength and strives to provide that to customers. In this case, all problems are solved within the context of level of quality. A third leader values market leadership as the best indicator of success. The knowledge workers in this organization will strive to make sales to boost market share before other factors. These goals and values drive the actions and decisions of organizational members.

A goal can lead to a value to support it, but a value can lead to a set of goals that are true to the value. Motivation is much more

> **How are your goals and values connected? Do they motivate you?**

likely if you are clear on what you are working toward and why you are working in this direction.

> *Lincoln, although having a very nondescript persona, came alive and engaged all who were listening to his speeches with simple logic and caring that could not be denied. There was no doubt that Lincoln's heart was with the people. He conveyed that sense when he talked.*

Thinking about goals and values in a structured way is an important step in laying the foundation for your mindset and narrative. Goals and values go together. Goals can uncover values, but values can lead to goals. Consider the following factors in setting your goals and values.

Activities, Interests, and Successes

> **Your activities, interests, and successes?**

Consider your activities, interests, and successes when setting goals and values. Analyze the four categories of goals and values, including personal, professional, community, and expertise, for insights and motivations that uncover the real you.

What are you good at doing? What do you like to do? What has been successful for you? What do you value? What goals do you have? Are you recognizing and using your strengths? Also, see how goals and values can be very close to each other. One person's goal could be another's value and vice versa. How you define your goals or values is not as important as making them complementary to each other and relevant to your strengths. Then they can provide consistent direction and motivation to your work and life. A goal of an easy life may not match with a value of rigidity or maybe rigidity will make an easy life. A goal of making money may not match with a value of compassion or maybe giving away your money is compassionate. And a goal of founding a famous bakery doesn't match with a dislike of baking unless you know an expert dessert chef. The goal of excelling in speed car racing doesn't match a value of a simple country life unless racing is a hobby in your rural domain. Goals and values complement each other when they support each other. That connection is a personal one and you have to define it individually for yourself.

Lincoln's speeches were short but resonated a sensitivity and earnestness that captured all who listened. He spoke as one of the people, not as a politician, preacher, or prosecutor. He spoke as one who was committed to serving. He believed in self-governing and he was eager to know what people thought they needed from him in order to self-manage their lives. Lincoln was demonstrating his values as he shared his goals for the country and its people.

Some sample goals might include individual satisfaction, growth, supporting others, quality of life, control, easy living, winning a contest, being an expert, changing the world, or building an empire. Some sample values might include honesty, humility, rigidity, compassion, self-sustainability, integrity, learning, dominance, or gravitas. As you can see, goals and values can complement each other. Good luck in considering them as they apply to you.

Readiness

As a human, you progress through stages of development as you grow and embark on various initiatives. Abraham Maslow, a renowned psychologist, has identified five stages of human development. His premise and research can be applied to life in general or to any/all work in a specific domain. These levels can indicate an individual's readiness for achieving a goal. Recognizing the sequence of these development stages helps to set goals and values accordingly. Consider the five stages described in Chapter 4 "Behavioral Concepts and Examples" and how they will help shape your goals. Goals can only be helpful or fulfilled if they are achievable. If your goal stretches beyond your current level of development, then the goal will not be feasible. For example, if you have no sense of belonging in a community, a goal of launching a new program for community members is probably not feasible. The goal of launching a new program would represent a self-actualizing effort, which is the ultimate and final stage of development. All other stages must be fulfilled before this final stage is feasible. The five levels of development can give insight into yourself and your current ability to achieve.

Status Quo Versus Learning

Goal seeking and work can be thought of in two ways, status quo or learning. Are you seeking to keep a status quo in place or are you seeking to learn about new and current conditions in order to make goals that are relevant to these new conditions? Status quo takes comfort in keeping activities the same even when changes have occurred. Learning seeks to clarify the new needs that come with new conditions. Perhaps there is wisdom in seeking some of both.

These two approaches confirm the importance of a learning mindset (Dweck 2016). Dweck concludes that everyone engages in both status quo and learning thinking. What you have learned previously through experiences should not be totally discounted as a rationale to keep the status quo. However, a learning approach to confirm that status quo is rational cannot be eliminated. It is the learning approach that has to come first in order to determine if you will proceed with a plan to learn or to maintain a status quo. Learning is always the premier consideration when setting a goal.

Learning Versus Performance

In an autonomous world, the most important clarification of goals is the difference between learning and performance. Dweck clarifies the distinction. Learning goals engage the growth and development process. Whether you win or lose, are successful or not, learning happens if you are open to it. Openness to learning means inquiring into and recognizing the value in an experience or a challenge. Analyzing the experience and the wisdom gained is a learning pursuit. Performance goals target winning something at a point in time. Sometimes a goal is just to learn and not to be the best. And sometimes the goal is to win a medal, a contest, or a high grade.

> **Do you always consider learning from relevant data and information when making a decision?**

If you only have a goal of winning, then you may not gain any learning in your efforts. Winning is a performance goal that, when met, can turn off an openness to learning. Conversely, if you only have a learning goal, there is no tangible outcome expected, but you have added to your knowledge base. A combination of learning and performance is the best approach to maximizing your work.

SJMS faculty defines their vision for their students in terms of learning competencies, not performance. They intend to equip their students with the tools for learning, not for achieving high positions or making lots of money.

Just recognizing that you are in pursuit of learning or performance/winning is a good start to creating your goals. You may want to win to gain access to another

Are you always in a winning mode or do you value learning sometimes?

opportunity, but you may want to learn about a situation in order to better align your efforts to win. A focus on learning provides the framework for what needs to happen to reach a goal, what needs to be learned, and what values will support that learning.

In college, were you focused on getting a grade or on learning something? In life, are you focused on earning money or building a path to a higher level position where you are in demand because of your learning and expertise? Is your elected representative interested in the status quo/performance of reelection or in learning about his constituents' current and evolving needs in order to serve them? Figure 5.1 shows an integration of performance and learning goals.

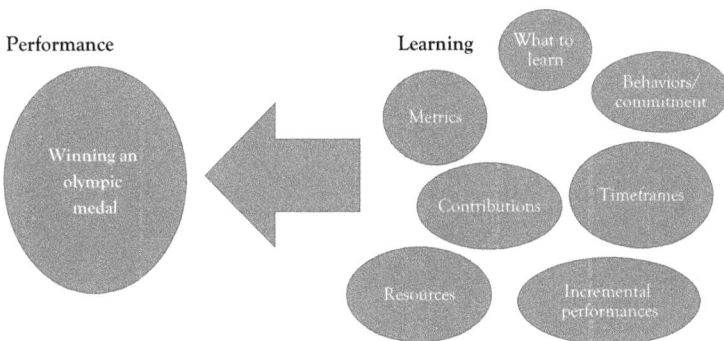

Figure 5.1 Integration of goals

Noah, (Interview with Frankel 2022), a technologist who founded a technology company, gained significant learning when he solicited new customers for his technology company. These potential customers didn't appreciate the unique value of customized software applications because they didn't understand the value to their own customers. Noah's employees also were not aware of the value of the usability features that his customized products provided. Noah's learning led him to create an incremental goal path to help his employees and customers recognize the tangible value of customized products. Achieving this goal would significantly propel his sales and company growth, as well as employees' understanding and commitment to the unique value of customized products.

Origins and Relevance of Your Goals and Values

The origins of your thinking helps to clarify the goals and values established in your life and whether that path is still relevant in current times and conditions. How have your nature and nurture, strengths, experiences, community mentality, and uncertainty shaped your thinking? Considering today's environment, your strengths, and your stage of development, is it relevant to continue with this path? If not, what should change? Include this analysis in forming your goals and values.

Hierarchy of Goals

Using passion to create goals should foster and include persistence in reaching your goals (Duckworth 2016). A goal can seem far away into the future but building a series of incremental goals helps to bring perspective to achieving your passion.

From an inner city and underprivileged neighborhood in Baltimore, Maryland, Wes Moore (https://wesmoore.com/about/) became a journalist and a citizen leader. He attended college and served in the U.S. military as a captain in Afghanistan. Also, after becoming a Rhoads Scholar, Moore led the Robin Hood Foundation to help people find opportunities to succeed. His vision was to give people opportunity to find a path to self-sufficiency. He believes that "no matter your start in life, you deserve an equal opportunity to succeed." His goal is found in that vision and he pursued it with the multiple service positions he has held in his life. He is serving as the Governor of Maryland, his home state....another step in his journey to fulfill that vision.

Moore's mindset is a great study in what you can achieve if open to exploration and incremental goal setting. His passion, goals, and value in self-sufficiency are rooted in his experiences and learning.

The hierarchy of mission goals in support of your vision is defined with a timeline, tracking, and pivoting, as needed. Think of the dimensions of your life and what you would like to achieve in your lifetime. Some incremental goals will be focused on learning and some on something tangible, a performance goal. Making a roadmap that includes both is helpful.

Using a hierarchy of goals recognizes incremental progress in achieving through learning (Duckworth 2016). This recognition will also keep you engaged, motivated, and satisfied while achieving each incremental goal toward longer-term ambitions. Also, incremental rewards reinforce persistence toward goal achievement. How might you reward yourself for persisting in achieving incremental goals?

Strengths

Your ambitions could and should be rooted in areas of your strengths, what you value, and your current stage of development and capability. Doing and excelling in what you are good at makes sense more than trying to develop skills and expertise in other areas. Usually, what you are good at is what you value. It is important to recognize that your goals actually connect to what you value and are good at. It is also important to recognize your current state and what you need to achieve on the way to your ultimate ambition, your destiny or legacy.

Alexander Hamilton's life started out in a bleak manner. With no parents by the age of 14, he knew he had to build something for himself. He managed to attract the attention of a newspaper editor with his writing skills to secure a trip to the new colony, America, for schooling. Social status was an issue as he was of mixed blood and had no real network of support from family or friends. Once in America, he found an opportunity to help George Washington as an aide, writing vital correspondence. His vision was to contribute to the making of America. His mission was to build opportunity for himself that would allow his vision to become reality. He eventually created the country's financial system that would support funding through banking, lending, and debt management. It was an unprecedented and unmatched system of great renown.

Hamilton didn't immediately pursue his ultimate goal, his vision, at an early age and low level of readiness (Maslow). He created a hierarchy of goals that would prepare him to achieve his legacy of helping to build America as an independent country. These goals maximized his strengths for himself and his country.

Consider Gardner's learning styles as strengths. Where are you strongest and how will that strength support your other efforts toward your passion. For example, a literary or communication strength can contribute to your message and narrative, which will undoubtedly move you through the stages of development needed to achieve your goals.

As previously noted, your strengths are your best asset. Keep them in mind as you plan your goals. Your strengths will help you reach all of your goals and should be integrated into all of your thinking and work. Why not leverage your best asset to propel you toward achieving all of your goals?

Give Direction

Hopefully, everyone has goals, ambitions, and passions. A vision is a passion, which is supported by your values and goals. Have you considered life at 50 years of age? What does your life look like at that point? Perhaps an ambition or passion can lead to some tangible and incremental goals to guide your pursuits and decisions? Many start-ups are founded on a passion of the founder. Following a person's ambition and/or passion makes persistence easier.

Your delight and joy in life are the best goals to pursue as they are easily related to your passion. This passion can lead to many and diverse areas of focus. If your passion is health care, there are many ways and areas in which you can fulfill goals with health care activities. If you feel motivated, satisfied, and in control when you are helping people learn, many industries and roles can be relevant platforms for this type of work.

Tom Brady, initially drafted in a later round of the football draft, knew the value of his passion that would lead to future contributions to an NFL team. Once drafted and upon meeting the team owner of the New England Patriots, Brady told him that he was the best thing that ever happened to this team. Brady had the confidence to make this statement because he knew his value and how to work to deliver that value. He was not boasting; he was just forecasting the future and he knew he could deliver on this expectation through his hierarchy of goals, both learning and performance in nature, that would lead his team to Superbowl success. Brady felt the passion driving his work and capacity to deliver on his goals as a superb quarterback.

Aligning Goals and Values to Each Other

Your values and goals can be defined together. If you know what you value, it is much easier to define your goals. If you know your goals, it is easy to uncover supportive values to ensure relevant work toward these goals. When you have not defined goals or values, it is questionable as to whether they are working in support of each other. This creates the risk that you are working against yourself. This conflict is apparent when decisions do not lead to good outcomes. When and if this happens, check for a gap in the alignment of your goals and values. If needed, consider whether it is best to change the goal or change the value.

Facebook, in a 2021 whistle-blower report (Kang and Mac 2021), was accused of valuing profits over people. Since approximately 52 percent of American adults get their news information in 2021 from Facebook, it would seem important that there was some filtering process to ensure the security of validity and credibility in postings. The report accuses Facebook of valuing money over the security of their product offering. Facebook's algorithmic decisions on what gets posted and what gets flagged are in question. If the accusation is true, this would be an example of a value and a goal in conflict. Facebook will tell you that it values the security of its users and then allows misinformation to appear on the user pages. Clearly, misinformation is not in the best security interest of Facebook users. This conflict could be an

unending source of trouble for Facebook, building resentment in its
user base, its employees, and its advertising clients.

Finally, are your goals and values those that will set the stage for your desired narrative? This last check is so important.

Goals and Feasibility

Finally, factors of your environment, your strengths, and your priorities will dictate how you balance your passion, purpose, profit, and productivity when making your goals. All goals are usually not achieved at the same time and some will even be compromised by a higher importance of another. The hierarchy of goals helps make progress feasible by prioritizing goals. This hierarchy can span all four categories of goals, as well as the learning and performance nature of goals. How do your goals relate to each other? Do they contribute to each other? Is learning in one area a factor for achievement in another?

Consider how your passion contributes to your purpose in life. Also think about how factors of profit and productivity contribute to that passion and purpose. With four categories to set goals, it is likely that you can include work and goals for each of these areas to complement each other. Compromise, incremental goals, persistence, and patience will allow you to find paths to satisfying and motivating yourself in all four of these areas. Perhaps the next few years are dedicated to establishing and achieving your area of expertise goals so that you can later focus on your professional goals. If your passion is foundational to your personal goals, you might consider working on your community goals in a way that serves your personal goals to expedite your progress. There are innumerable ways to plan achievement in a feasible manner with complementary compromise and prioritization as facilitating perspectives.

Categories of Goals

Four categories of goals/values can be considered to support your growth and development. Consider a vision and mission for each category:

- **Personal**—What would you like to achieve during the long term of your life? What values will support these goals?

- **Professional**—What would you like to achieve during your total career? What values will support these goals?
- **Community**—What would you like to contribute to any communities to which you belong? What values will support these goals?
- **Expertise**—What specific skills do you wish to master in your lifetime? What does your narrative include? What values will support these goals?

You don't have to define all these goals and values at one time. Focus might be on one category at a time, but they will likely overlap and be aligned to support each other.

Let's explore each category.

Personal and Professional Goals/Values

Personal and professional goals give comfort, context, and confidence. What are your personal ambitions? What quality of life are you seeking? Who do you aspire to become as a person? What led you to this vision for your destiny and legacy? What do you aspire to achieve professionally? What do you want your last job in life to look like? What will you have achieved to secure that job? How do your personal goals align with these professional goals? How do you want others to think of you as a person? As a professional?

Now consider the values that will help you achieve your personal and professional goals. They are as important as the goals themselves as they are enablers to achievement.

Community Goals/Values

Depending on the communities to which you belong, you will create goals and values as they relate to that organization and its vision, goals, and values. You can match your strengths and values to the community and plan contributions accordingly. What does this community strive to achieve? What are their strengths and what do they need that you might contribute? What are your strengths and contributions that might add new value to that community? You can also fulfill goals and values of your own with this contribution. These contributions will add to your narrative and should be considered in that context, as well.

When working within a community, it is best to consider the mindsets of the community members, as well as that of the community itself. As in all cases, stakeholder alignment is essential to success. It is best to create a common set of goals and values.

> *Damien, a young tennis player, considered the goals and values of his friends and those of the members of the tennis academy. Clearly, the goals and values of those at the tennis academy were a better match for his goal of becoming a professional tennis player. He moved himself to the environment that would best serve his ambitions, as well as allow him to contribute to the tennis community to which he wanted to belong.*

Goals and Values for Your Expertise

Your expertise is foundational to your confidence, growth, and narrative. What do you want that expertise to be? What strengths will you use? How will you establish it, and what goals will guide your success in that domain? The narrative of your expertise follows you and is integral to other's desire to work with you and value your contributions. What do you value that contributes to and supports your expertise? The goals and values of your expertise are a significant part of your narrative. Figure 5.2 summarizes the goals structure.

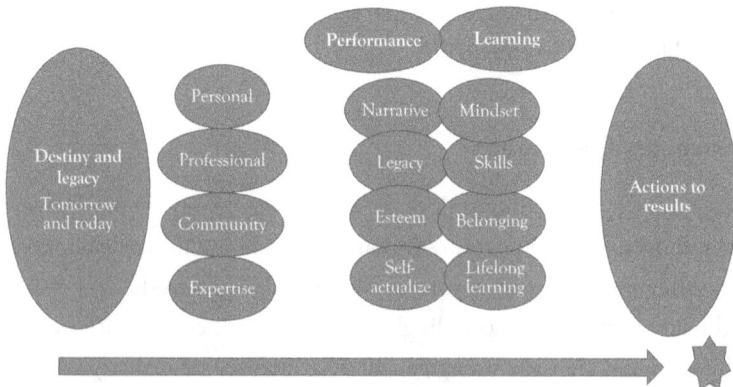

Figure 5.2 Goals structure

Daily Goals and Values, Daily Work

Thinking about the outcome of every effort before it is undertaken provides a guide for decisions that will lead to an anticipated outcome, as well as aligning to the goal hierarchy for set up of the next goal and its achievement. How will a task contribute to a higher-level goal? Is it aligned? Recognizing your daily goals as learning or performance will help with identifying and achieving a relevant outcome for all work toward a higher goal.

Profiling

Making a profile for yourself will help you define your goals, values, and narrative. Consider the following for your profile:

1. Your expertise
2. Value proposition
3. Experiences
4. Goals: vision and mission
5. Values
6. Growth plans
7. Passion
8. Narrative
9. Support for collaborators

> **Caution: If you are not clear on your goals and values, someone else will set them for you.**

Defining Your Desired Narrative

The outcome of your mindset and work is your narrative, which is your brand, your story. Your narrative is told through the artifacts of your behaviors and decisions. What do you want stakeholders to say about you? Stakeholders hold impressions of you, thus, making your narrative a reality for them. Artifacts provide evidence of your narrative, which is made up of the characteristics that others see when considering you and how you work.

Do your goals and values support the narrative you would like your stakeholders to hold of you? Goals might include a significant win of a contract, to meet a deadline, or to become informed about a new industry. Values might include inquiry, research, collaboration, or customer satisfaction.

The story to be told could be one of helpfulness, camaraderie, persistence, and results-orientation. It could also indicate self-interest, a priority on maximizing profits, or meeting shareholder, as opposed to stakeholder, needs. What is the narrative that you would like the world to believe about you? How do your goals and values support this narrative? How do others see you? If they don't hold this narrative of you, what needs to change? Figure 5.3 summarizes these narrative perspectives.

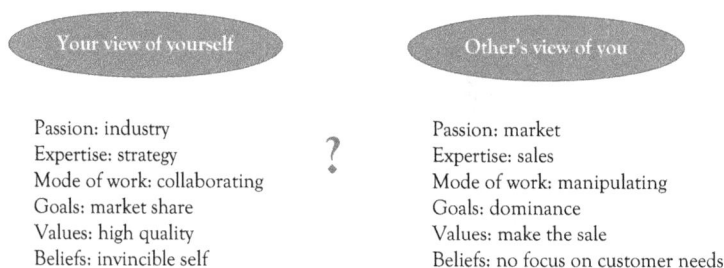

Your view of yourself		Other's view of you
Passion: industry	?	Passion: market
Expertise: strategy		Expertise: sales
Mode of work: collaborating		Mode of work: manipulating
Goals: market share		Goals: dominance
Values: high quality		Values: make the sale
Beliefs: invincible self		Beliefs: no focus on customer needs

Figure 5.3 Matching narrative perspectives

Lincoln understood where influence was strongest. He was a pragmatist and an idealist. When he could sense that he could influence a change, he made that effort. When decision makers were not open to a change, he held back until he could see a victory on the horizon. He did not attempt a change when others were more influential than he could be.

Lincoln worked hard on his narrative, especially with the common man and soldiers who were fighting the Civil War. His views were contrary to his fellow politicians in many cases, but he continued to treat them with respect and attempts to win them over to his point of view. His values were rooted in freedom for all and this was not a popular perspective with many of the elite who were his peers. In some ways, Lincoln was above the common politics of his day and was respected by some and disrespected by others. He was persistent in his narrative that supported freedom for all. No one was confused about his intent.

Observing Others

Observing others gives you two important clues to uncovering a narrative, either of yourself or of someone else. First, keep in mind that narratives are created from your own mindset. Often you project your own mindset on to others and can entirely misjudge a motive or rationale of another's behavior or mode of work. The frame of reference is that of your own mindset. When you perceive a negative motivation from someone's behavior, it is often because you have that same motivation yourself. If you are judging another's behavior, consider why you think the way that you do.

Secondly, when defining or refining your own narrative, it is often helpful to observe others' behaviors. Do these behaviors mimic your own? And what do you think of that person based on that behavior? Do you like what you see or do you find those behaviors distasteful? They could be a clue to your own behaviors, how others observe you, and how you want others to see you. Often you are not aware of how a behavior appears to others. Observing others' behaviors and the narrative these behaviors cre-

> My purpose in life is to…..
> (what to achieve) in a way
> that…..(factors to achieve
> and mindset to be used) so
> that…..(result to achieve).

ate can help with insights into yourself as you might be seen by others (Brooks 2021). By evaluating others, you can gain insights into what others might see in you. Consider a narrative statement for yourself in the following format.

Intended Narrative and Actual Narrative

A narrative accompanies each of us automatically. It may or may not be what you intend when you state your values and beliefs. What is your narrative? What actions and behaviors validate it? Based on your goals and ability to meet them, do you need to alter your behaviors and decisions in order to support this narrative? How do others define it? If and when you are working with others, which is mostly always in a knowledge economy, it really only matters how others define your narrative. You are dependent on your stakeholders to be successful in your work so the narrative they hold of you is important for you to manage. Does your own narrative match that of another's perception of it? How does that narrative match with your own version of it? These questions will build deep awareness of your own narrative, how others view it, and how narratives can foster high levels of joint productivity.

Awareness of others and their narratives also gives you insights into those who can potentially offer complementary work to your own. People can be dependent on others not only for needed resources but also for ideas for viable projects and value creation. Sharing a narrative is a significant first step in effective collaboration.

Does your intended narrative meet your actual narrative? Clarity on this point brings clarity to your mindset and how it serves your activity and decisions. If your actions and decisions are not accepted as you would like them to be by your colleagues or stakeholders, perhaps your narrative is not what you think it is. Checking others' perceptions can lead to a more realistic concept of self and guide changes that will tell your story differently. Behaviors and decisions can be changed if you are aware of them and what they need to be.

Reinforcing and Managing Your Intended Narrative

Reinforcing your narrative happens through the continuous reflection on outcomes, intended and actual. When there is a gap, there is a danger of rendering your narrative ineffective or, perhaps, even causing damage to yourself or your organization. Checking for gaps between your actual and intended narrative should provide insights into how and why the gap occurred and how to restore your narrative to its intended state.

A gap can occur for multiple reasons, not all negative. Perhaps a goal is unrealistic or a partner has a different goal. Restoring a narrative might just be a matter of clarifying for stakeholders the reason for the gap or lack of success. Researching the cause of a gap could be a good joint project for those involved, clarifying mismatches along the way and finding fixes that will maintain the value of your positive narrative.

Stakeholders, their needs, and their narrative of you can change with different projects. Stakeholders, as has been noted previously, have a major role in forming your narrative, in conveying it to the world, and expecting it when working with you. It is their perception of you that contributes to the forming of your narrative. When asked, they will share that perception with others. And that perception of your narrative will dictate how and if they will choose to work with you in a positive collaboration.

Keeping track of your mindset drivers and your narrative is a never-ending pursuit. Following are some topics to consider in this pursuit.

Aligning Goals and Values to Your Desired Narrative

Now that you have identified your desired narrative, make sure that your goals and values support that narrative. Consider characteristics of the narrative that you desire and match to related goals and values. Do these goals and values match your own?

Aligning goals, values, and a desired narrative is the best way to be sure that you are communicating your intended message. Goals and values guide your work and thinking, which convey your narrative. Lack of alignment creates distrust and confusion, which doesn't help your path to success.

> **What narrative do you want the world to have of you? What goals and value will spark that narrative?**

Defining and Aligning to Organizational and Stakeholder Goals and Values

Understanding your organization's and stakeholder's profiles helps with context for meeting your individual goals and values. Do you often think differently than your leader, organization, or partner? Does the leader not see the value in what you present or an idea that you think is brilliant? Organizational, stakeholder, and individual goals and values should match for efficient work to prevail. Consider profile information for a match to your individual and your organizational goals and values. Consider stakeholder profiles, as well, for indicators of the stakeholders' goals and values? How do they match with your own? Your organization's? Where do you need to consider refinements or modifications to strengthen the match?

Consider the following characteristics to define your organization and stakeholders:

- Industry, market
- Value proposition
- Customer profile
- Goals: vision and mission
- Values
- Growth plans
- Passion
- Narrative
- Support for collaborators
- Environment for autonomy

Now match these characteristics to your individual goals and values in your profile. Where do you need a better match? What can you change to strengthen that match?

You must consider your organization's and stakeholders' goals and value when planning your work. How will your goals and values impact the organization and stakeholders? How will their goals and values impact your own goals and values? Where and how might you ensure a common platform for working together?

At each step in the hierarchy of goals, there will be tasks to be completed and stakeholders to engage. Will your goals and values continue to be realistic when considering their goals and values?

Organizational and Stakeholder Narratives

An organizational narrative is built through shared experiences when working within the organization. Organizational leaders create the environment that supports knowledge workers and these workers tell the story of the organization. Organizational goals and values set the platform for this environment. The organization's goals and values become everyone's as they work together. Stakeholders build narratives in the same way and should be considered accordingly.

Worksheet Reference

Worksheets to facilitate using the concepts in this chapter are found in "Developing the Intentional Mindset, Module 3: Setting Goals and Values." The worksheets include:

Setting Your Goals
Understanding Your Values
Goals and Values Alignment
Hierarchy of Goals
Aligning Individual, Organizational, and Stakeholder Goals and Values

Call to Action

Considering your life and activities in the last five years, define who you are and what you strive to achieve.

1. Consider the quality of life you desire, your current strengths and expertise, and your compensation needs to support your quality of life.
2. Consider the narrative that you would like to have as your story to the world.
3. Set your goals and values for all four categories: personal, professional, community, and expertise to contribute to that narrative. Plan and test their feasibility by comparing, aligning, and prioritizing them together for easiest achievement.
4. Describe the organization and stakeholders you would like to engage for fulfilling your goals and values.
5. Consider the timeline for each of your goal and value categories.
6. Consider what you will join, read, or access as resources to keep currently informed in relevant areas. How will you create your environment for success with alignment of goals and values, yours and/or others, as well as find opportunities for learning?
7. Make a plan of action for each of these goals and value categories.
8. Plan tracking of progress with relevant metrics and measures.
9. Reflect, refine, and reconfirm your goals and values as they contribute to your narrative.

Chapter Summary

This chapter helps you to define your goals and values, as well as align them to each other and to the goals and values of your stakeholders and organization. The next chapter helps you connect your goals and value to your beliefs (biases) and mode of work. It also helps you to align these beliefs and mode of work to those of your stakeholders and organization.

CHAPTER 6

Connecting Goals and Values to Beliefs and Mode of Work

A 2014 program, Project-based Internships, at a large urban university in Philadelphia, PA, sought to build trust and relationships between the emerging workforce members and the regional work community. These

| Behaviors and mode of work reflect your goals and values and create your narrative. Recognizing and managing your narrative is critical. |

work organizations had a need for work to be done. The program structured the work as a project so that the students' experience built an understanding of how mindset is set and knowledge work is done. The hosting companies gained a tangible outcome of the work based on the goals and values of the organization. The students gained an understanding of how they and their skills could contribute to the organizations' needs. An analysis of the benefits achieved along with the impact that those benefits created was completed by the students and reviewed by the hosting company sponsor. Once the project work was completed and reviewed by the organization leader, many of these students were offered positions to continue working within the organizations. Trust, relationship, and stakeholdership had been developed by each for the other. They had developed a common mindset for the work that was to be achieved.

Once goals and values have been defined, aligned with each other, and confirmed with organizational and stakeholder perspectives, it is now time to move onto exploring the beliefs and modes of work that demonstrate those goals and values as you work. Your beliefs, resulting behaviors, and mode of work are your tangible connection to your organization and stakeholders. How you are perceived creates their narrative of you. That narrative can be the most critical aspect of your success.

Beliefs, behaviors, and mode of work are often implicit and unconscious. They may or may not support the goals and values that you have articulated. It is important that they not only algin so that you are working in support of yourself but also so that people see those connections and view you as credible. If one is not credible, working with others as is necessary in the knowledge economy is difficult, if not impossible. One cannot work well with a noncredible narrative. This alignment, also, makes it much easier for you to work effectively to reach a goal. When they match, you are not working against your goals and values.

When beliefs and modes of work are implicit or unconscious, you have to work hard to uncover them. Consider your successes and failures, as well as others' reactions to your work, to help identify a good alignment of your goals and values to your beliefs and modes of work.

Wondering why your ideas are not meeting with approval or even consideration? Sometimes your stakeholders are not interested. But why? What is their perspective of you and your work? Perhaps they just have other original ideas that serve their own purposes? Or maybe your ideas make no sense to them? Is it your idea or the idea of working with you that is an issue here? Are you confusing people when your values don't seem to match your behaviors?

> **Do you connect your goals and value with your beliefs and mode of work?**

These queries can help you understand the importance of your aligned mindset, as well as its match to collaborators. This chapter discusses aligning your goals and values with your beliefs and mode of work and, then, aligning both to your collaborators.

The key ideas in this chapter include:

- Defining and aligning current beliefs and mode of work
- Understanding and aligning organizational beliefs, mode of work, goals and values

- Aligning all stakeholders' mindsets and work
- Working together: techniques for matching mindsets

Defining and Aligning Current Beliefs and Mode of Work

Beliefs are the tenets of goals and values that drive our behaviors and mode of work. Beliefs translate goals and values into everyday actions. If beliefs are not aligned and supportive of your goals and values, your behaviors and mode of work will cause confusion and obstruct progress. Uncertainty of beliefs, behaviors, and decisions make people unproductive as it delays action and creates fear of the consequences of unacceptable behaviors and outcomes.

Beliefs as Biases—Intended and Implicit

Beliefs can be thought of as opinions, assumptions, or biases. They are based on origins that we can explore. Refer to Chapter 3 "Origins of a Mindset" for a description of these origins of nature and nurture, strengths, experiences, community mentality, and uncertainties. Recognizing people's beliefs as opinions, assumptions, or biases, both implicit and explicit, is important. Explicit biases are beliefs that are within your awareness. Implicit biases happen without your awareness. It is easier to change the explicit biases, but not impossible to change the implicit biases that obstruct progress toward an expected outcome. Once you have identified the belief or bias with the *Five Whys*, you can identify its origin and consider how to change a belief, as needed, for better outcomes of your work.

Beliefs have a direct influence and impact on decisions and are especially critical when they are not aligned with your goals and values. If you want to provide help to a group of immigrants, your bias about their lack of sophistication or intelligence will not build their trust and relationship with you. If you believe that another person is trying to discredit you, you may not be able to build trust, relationship, or stakeholdership with that person. No progress will prevail toward your goal. It is helpful to identify and modify these biases before allowing them to direct your behaviors and decisions for failure.

Beliefs have impacts that may be unexpected. Awareness of the belief and its impact can help you refine the belief to be more aligned with your goals and values. This awareness can be developed in two ways: observing people's reactions and reflecting on the unexpected outcome. We often don't know what we don't know. You can self-diagnose a belief by looking at your behaviors and decisions that are driven by that belief. Does the outcome meet expected results? Why is a result not as expected? What belief caused a behavior or decision, your own or others', that caused the result? This belief and subsequent result needs to be explored to clarify its impact causing the unexpected failure or success.

> **What do you believe that is not a fact?**

Mode of Work

Mode of work is how you work. It includes organizational protocols defined by the expectations of the leader of an organization and by the knowledge worker's individual values and beliefs. Some examples of modes of work include routine practices, such as timelines, access to data and information, and human resources; decision-making and communication protocols; team efforts; and sharing of goals, values, and growth expectations. Individual and organizational modes of work should match for creating the common platform for efficiency and effectiveness of work. Examples of modes of work, such as mindset awareness, learning and inquiry, and autonomy in decision making, are detailed in Chapter 2 "Defining Mindset Components."

> **Can you describe how you work individually? With others?**

Building a Narrative

Connecting and aligning goals and values to beliefs and mode of work build an intentional narrative for achievement of desired outcomes. This connection and alignment create the narrative that tells your story to the world. A person who espouses a value and then doesn't back it up with supporting beliefs and mode of work is not trusted or followed very well. A narrative tells this story as it is grounded in your mindset. Recognizing this important link is essential in conveying the narrative you desire. This mindset drives a large percentage of your decisions, so you want it to be functional and credible and a solid foundation for your narrative. Once you have worked through the goals and values of your mindset, you will want to build the beliefs and mode of work that will demonstrate them to the world in your narrative.

Beware that creating your narrative based on your mindset is not finite. It has to be rethought as conditions change, as you grow and develop throughout your life, and as you work on various projects.

Martin Posth (Posth 2006) was the Volkswagen AG head of a joint venture with the Chinese to enhance their automotive industry with Volkswagen products, which was the goal of both parties. Posth's narrative had to portray him as an advocate for the Chinese for the partnership to work. He had to demonstrate understanding of what and how the Chinese were thinking. The Chinese had no background in Western thinking or work. They were totally naive in partnering so he would have to patiently bring them along to understanding Western ways. Western management awareness and practices had to be built with every conflicting thought that came up on a daily basis. His narrative needed to convey an openness to convince the Chinese how to work for the improved automotive industry that they sought together.

Confirmation and Desirability Belief

Often people seek to confirm their mindsets with data and information that support their current thoughts or desires, not necessarily their goals and values. This need for confirmation of what you currently think can invalidate your stated goals and values. Confabulations can create a lack of reality and rationale and skew beliefs and modes of work to be detrimental to your success. Alignment to your goals and values can become difficult. Also, this is not a positive way to build trust and relationship into your narrative. Considering how you would like to be remembered or what you wish to accomplish in your life, personally, professionally, for your community, and in the domain of your expertise, can build awareness of the confirmation discrepancy and rationalization. Dispelling this need for confirmation will open the path to create the mindset that will lead to a positive and accurate narrative of you in the world. Goals and values really need to be demonstrated by your beliefs and mode of work. You are now working with the mindset that will support you effectively.

Aligning to Goals and Values

Most important is that your beliefs and mode of work are aligned with your goals and values. If they are not, your outcomes will not be certain. If you believe unconditionally in the righteousness of your answers and approach, then the value that others have to contribute to a joint decision will be lost. Their motivation to contribute at all will be compromised, resulting in failure to reach an expected outcome. If a leader believes that people constantly need direction because they cannot make decisions on their own, then his mode of work will reflect this belief with lots of micro-management. If that same leader is touting a goal of independence and a value of individual growth, his mode of work is in conflict and will not be credible. The leader will not be viewed as honest. People will not be motivated to contribute to the organization's goals and values. Their path to growth has been compromised by his approach.

Following are some beliefs and modes of work. Consider the goals and values that might be demonstrated by these beliefs and modes of work. Consider and complete Table 6.1 for a sample matching of mindset components.

Table 6.1 Matching mindset components

Belief/Bias	Behavior/Mode of Work	Goals	Values
Others' value is equally important to my own.	Always listen before deciding	Maximizing performance	Humility
Deviations are not good.	Predetermine a behavior before understanding circumstances	Complete control	Rigidity
All is OK all the time.	No action to resolve anything because all is OK	...	...
Identifying truth is essential.	Determination to pin down the facts	...	...

Belief/Bias	Behavior/Mode of Work	Goals	Values
Valuing others over self is most effective.	Compassionate action to help in any way possible	...	...
Pleasing yourself first is essential.	Serve your own needs before considering impact to another	...	...
Do the right thing over all else.	Righteous choice over convenience or loss	...	...
Adapting goals and values to accommodate any outcome at all costs is effective.	Minimizing impact as fits your desires for your own outcomes	...	...
Pleasant behavior endears you to anyone for any purpose.	Polite exchanges in all interactions	...	...
Spend as little as possible on all work.	Do not contribute your fair share	...	...
Curiosity is never overrated.	Zeal in questioning and seeking information	...	...
You must be in charge of all that involves you.	Arrogant responses, no consulting on decisions	...	...
Another?	Another?	...	...

Defining Your Beliefs and Mode of Work

Defining your beliefs and mode of work is easiest when you begin by matching them to your goals and values. What beliefs and mode of work would you expect to deliver in support of those goals and values? It is also helpful to consider recent work and its outcomes. Unexpected outcomes, positive or negative, provide invaluable clues to your actual beliefs and mode of work. A process of scientific inquiry can examine the relationship between a belief or decision and the rationale of a goal or value that led to either of them. The *Five Whys* approach allows a systematic analysis of this connection. Why did you choose a behavior or decision? Why did you believe that? Why did you believe or value that? Why did you...? Why did you...? Eventually you will understand the source/rationale or your belief or decision. Also, your organization's and stakeholders' beliefs must be considered for collaborative and expedient work toward a common goal. Are your beliefs aligned with your goals and values, as needed, and to those of your organization and stakeholders? Even more important is exploring the origin of beliefs and mode of work to help in making a change, if needed, for better outcomes. Table 6.2 summarizes a sample conclusion of an analysis.

Table 6.2 Mindset analysis and alignment

Recent Work	Belief, Mode of Work, Outcome	Goal and Origin	Values and Origin
Setting up a research team	Belief: Research is good. Mode of Work: Assigning member participation Outcome: Lack of interest	Collaboration for learning and growth; supporting learning environment	Research-based decisions; science background
Five Whys Conclusion on Alignment: The outcome doesn't contribute to the goal because the mode of work is not aligned with the goal of collaboration, even though the belief and values are aligned.			
Creating a new revenue stream	Belief: Growth is essential. Mode of work: Growth team to facilitate and reward ideas and opportunities Outcome: Numerous quantified and qualified options for growth	Organizational intrapreneuring; seeking the validation of self-esteem	Supporting innovative activity with a digital nervous system and resources; experienced in assessment and validation
Five Whys Conclusion on Alignment: The outcome is as expected due to an aligned platform of matching goal, value, belief, and mode of work.			

Now you can identify where you might be able to change something, such as a goal, a value, or a belief, that would allow a better decision. This is, also, an opportunity to find a link to a common thought among adversaries and their values or beliefs. Figure 6.1 shows the relationship between goals, values, beliefs, and mode of work.

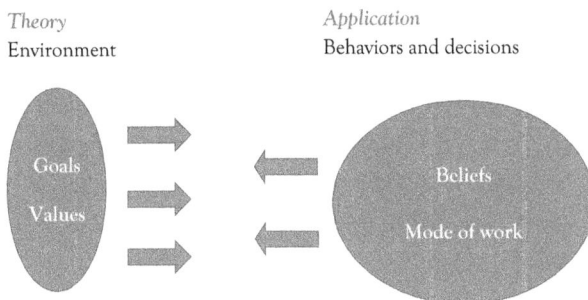

Figure 6.1 Goals and values relating to beliefs and mode of work

Posth of VW encountered mismatches of beliefs with VW headquarters and his Chinese partners. At a technical status meeting there was disagreement about an advisory fee to be paid by the Chinese to the German parent company. In China, advising means asking a question and getting an answer, it is free. In Germany, there is a fee for advisory services. The Chinese and Posth thought the advisory fee was unfair. They agreed on this instance of differing values, agreeing to disagree with German headquarters.

This instance occurred because there was a lack of understanding of the Chinese by the Germans and the same for the Chinese understanding of the Germans. Posth observed that you cannot expect to work across intercultural boundaries without changing yourself in the process, as well as having expectations that your partners will change.

Helping the Chinese mindset shift from a state-driven to a market-driven model was challenging. Posth found ways to use all four of Grant's communication/discussion personas of preacher, prosecutor, politician, and scientific inquirer to make his case for a market-driven environment and build trust with his Chinese partners.

Posth had to compromise Western goals and deadlines. If Posth's goal was to create a working partnership in the timeframe expected, he did not meet it. His values lay elsewhere. Wolfsburg headquarters would tell you that they value timely meeting of deadlines but Posth actually valued collaboration more than deadlines. Posth also had to deal with Chinese built-in mistrust of foreigners due to colonial Europeans and their tyranny in previous centuries. He resorted to building trust through a common platform of goals for the initiative. Posth built the needed commitment to collaboration with continuous reminders of those goals. Although Chinese leaders had a goal of benefitting from the Western standardized performance parameters set by the Germans, they cringed when the Germans actually implemented them. Posth had to refine this Chinese goal to one of achieving the enhanced Chinese automotive industry. Posth saw the wisdom in moving from the process goal of mastering German performance to one of enhancing the Chinese automotive industry. Everyone was on board with that common goal.

Understanding and Aligning Organizational Beliefs, Mode of Work, Goals, and Values

Most effective work happens when an individual and project or organization are aligned in mindset. Consider a recent project to gain insight and clarity of a project or organizational mindset.

Living standards in China were vastly different than those that German or American expatriates might expect. As needed VW experts, they would have to be convinced of the value of relocating to China for a time. Beliefs in what you need and want would have to be clarified in the context of the value of what was to be achieved. A belief that living with less conveniences was necessary for working for a common goal with the Chinese had to be established.

Project and/or Organizational Mindset

Once you have established your own beliefs and mode of work as they align with your goals and values, it is important to evaluate how they fit with those of your organization. Consider your organization's characteristics and how they translate into beliefs and mode of work. Individual projects can also have their own characteristics, beliefs, and mode of work. A match among all

> **How do you describe your organization's beliefs and mode of work?**

of these entities is necessary for efficient and effective work toward the common goal. What changes might you need to your own mindset to accommodate your organization's or a project's beliefs and mode of work? Queries that might shed light on this alignment include:

- What are your project/organization's beliefs and values?
- How do they match your own beliefs and values?
- What can you realign for making a better match for successful work?

Aligning All Stakeholders' Mindsets and Work

Stakeholders are anyone who can support, contribute to, or derail your project or work. They may be an integral part of your work or they may be on the sidelines, advising or just observing. They can be internal, external, indirect, direct, and/or future influencers on your work. Stakeholders are able to impact the outcomes of your work directly and indirectly. Identifying them and their influences or impacts allow you to manage them by accommodating and aligning with their mindset needs.

Posth thought about the potential outcomes of the behaviors of the Chinese employees. No one in China wants to take responsibility. It is a fearful thing to them. He would have to help them feel safe to take the responsibility to make decisions when needed. Basic management techniques were not known in China, so Wolfsburg sent in management trainers to provide a program to establish management skills and comfort with making needed decisions.

In another context, VW's contributing engineers have a very distinct community mentality. They are trained to follow the directions of the schematic. There are no questions or discussions necessary. They are not known to be good communicators and when the Chinese want to understand and give an opinion on every detail of an installation of a machine, the engineers are not comfortable with these Chinese needs. Every Chinese worker needs to have his input. Posth facilitates this mismatch by overcoming Chinese mistrust, fear, and ignorance so they could accept the engineers' work without question.

For stakeholders to support or contribute to your work, mindsets must be in common. If goals differ, work is oriented in differing directions. What beliefs and decisions are a good fit with others as your stakeholders? If you can identify these matches, then you can design your work to accommodate both stakeholder and your own needs simultaneously. Queries that might shed light on this alignment include:

- Who are the stakeholders on whom you depend to contribute to your actions and decisions? What are their individual levels of influence?
- What are their mindsets?
- What narrative do they hold of you and your mindset? Is it aligned with your personal narrative of yourself?
- What changes will be needed to match?

Can you describe your stakeholders' beliefs and modes of work?

The most straightforward way to reach this common mindset platform of work is to engage a common goal. When all workers are aligned in this context, it becomes easier to align supporting values, beliefs, and mode of work.

Prioritizing Project Stakeholders With Levels of Influence

Once all stakeholders have been identified for a specific project, it is important to recognize their levels of influence on your project. Stakeholders may be of high influence or low influence. But all stakeholders are in need of your concern to be sure that their needs are met and not creating an obstacle to your endeavors. The question of how important a stakeholder is to your pursuit is of upmost importance. If it includes funding to continue your work, then that stakeholder will require a different level of your attention and accommodation than one who is not integral to your work, such as merely needing to be informed of your progress. Once identified, a stakeholder should be rated in influence and prioritized accordingly for your attention.

What are the mindset characteristics of those stakeholders who could support or adversely affect your project? Consider the impact of their goals, values, beliefs, and mode of work on your project and its goals? How do these need to be accommodated or changed to ensure their support?

> **What mindset obstacles have derailed a recent project?**

Working Together: Techniques for Matching

Work that is aligned with a common platform of mindset has a high likelihood of success. When mindset components seem aligned but work is meeting difficulties, there are numerous techniques to consider that will help identify and create the alignment needed to move forward and reach goals together. They are described in the following.

Reaching Agreement: Go Back to Goals

Differing mindset components often result in conflicts and obstacles to moving forward with intended work toward a stated goal. Returning to the common goal and seeking compromise on how work is viewed and completed to meet the goal is a sure way to move forward (Posth 2006). Questions for discussion include:

1. What is the common goal?
2. What is the benefit to each stakeholder?
3. Where are the mindset obstacles?
4. What is each willing to invest in reaching that goal?
5. What is the balance of that investment with the new value to be created when you reach the common goal?

Brainsteering and mind mapping sessions will help all to agree on changes to get on the same path to continue work.

Lincoln had a huge and complex task at hand. The new country needed to remain one entity in order to grow to its potential as a world leader for freedom and to provide every man the ability to grow and create his own destiny. Eventually, the goal of growth tied people to a common effort to try to convince nonbelievers in the cause of freedom.

Plan Original Research, as Needed

Sometimes identifying a stakeholder's mindset is complex and not easily done. There is always the option of designing and conducting your own survey to identify specific characteristics of goals, values, beliefs, modes of work, and decisions. You can then use these data as a resource for building a common mindset. Profiles, origins of mindset, and narratives can be uncovered from this research, as well, and are very useful in meeting or altering a stakeholder's needs.

Listening

A proven technique for learning about others is the art of listening. Often, in today's accelerated times, you are distracted from listening in order to prepare a response to another's thought or challenge during discussions. Obviously, this is not effective listening, if listening at all.

> *The Barnes Foundation (Salisbury 2020) of Philadelphia, PA, offered a program to help physicians' assistants better connect to their patients. The program included very deep analyses of the Foundation's paintings, their clues, and messages of deep meaning. The physicians' assistants were then better able to explore the uncovered needs of their end-of-life patients to understand how to best accommodate their desires and values.*

There are many ways to listen that enhance or clarify what you think you know about a stakeholder, including:

- Words that are used give insight into a deeper level of importance or meaning.
- Tone of voice provides a sense of feelings.
- Body language signals inner sensitivities about a topic or another person.
- References to various scenarios or things give some context around another's thinking.
- Actions/behaviors tell the real story of another's goals, values, and beliefs.
- Decisions confirm another's real goals, values, and beliefs.

Lincoln was adamant in the concept of the "doctrine of instructions."
He was consistently clear on the essential nature of representation of
the will of the people. And he listened to those voices to guide the
intent of his work and voting pattern. He believed that people should
reap the rewards of their will and labor and worked to create the
country funding and institutions to allow this.

An astute listener can read between the lines of another's dialogue, often gaining more information than from the conversation itself. When building trust and relationship, listening intently can be very valuable. Often people say what is expected but don't really express their true feelings, values, and/or beliefs. Deep listening helps decipher true thoughts to guide further clarifying inquiry.

Workflow and Archetype Analyses

Archetypes of workflow and outcomes (Kleiner, Roberts, Ross, Senge, and Smith 1994) can be used to forecast problems in achieving expected outcomes. They help you identify gaps and obstacles in workflows in the context of these archetypes, which identify gaps in inputs and outputs caused by misalignment of goals, values, beliefs, behaviors, and/or modes of work. Once a gap is identified, it can be resolved with two tools to align current mindsets for better outcomes (Thaler and Sunstein 2008). These tools, decision influencers and choice architectures, provide additional and relevant information to alter mindsets to fill the gaps. Decision influencers include relevant data and information that reflect on a situation or current mindset. Considering new data or information often leads to new thoughts and can influence your own or a stakeholder's thinking. Choice architectures build scenarios to facilitate a choice for you or the stakeholder. These scenarios are positioned as choices of behaviors, actions, or decisions that each lead to a different outcome. The scenarios minimize decision making when perceived as overwhelming. It is a packaged and facilitated approach to decision making.

Archetypes, decision influencers, and choice architectures are described in detail in Chapter 7 "Ensuring Inquiry with a Learning System."

Aligning to Change—Individual, Organizational, Stakeholder

Beware that change advises mindsets and mindsets advise change. Goals and values can change as conditions change. The most recent 21st century changes in lifestyles present the need to value autonomy and self-sufficiency. The 21st century work needs have changed from previous eras where most workers were directed on exactly what they needed to do in their work to a more autonomous model based on the availability of data and information for decision making. Global relationships have created a need for new understandings of diverse mindsets, as well.

The climate crisis has made changes to how energy is used, what energy is used, and context for requiring new energy-saving behaviors. Technology updates are unrelenting as they continuously modify the expectations on how work gets done. Learning new programming languages and applications and digital literacy are continuous challenges. Culture changes, individual experiences, capability requirements, and family or social changes occur as examples of the continuously challenging and accelerated world that you live in. Therefore, mindsets have to change to accommodate changes that bombard everyone on a regular basis. These changes impact yourself, your organization, and your stakeholders. Recognizing and aligning the impact of changes among all of these constituents is more than challenging but should be considered in order to work within the current and continuously changing environment.

It is obvious that when change has to be accommodated, a value on learning has to be front and center in your thinking. It has to lay the foundation for managing the changes that inevitably make up your future. Inquiry and learning are values that are often touted but not always practiced. All activity should have inquiry and learning integrated for meaningful outcomes to occur. The knowledge economy provides the resources necessary to engage any and all inquiry for relevant learning in all activity. There is no end to the value and power of the untethered and voluminous data and information available to answer the right questions.

Communication

No one achieves anything alone. Communication is a necessary component of rallying and aligning contributors. You are dependent on others to enable your pursuits. Even when you eat breakfast alone, you are dependent on the food being available, the shelter in which you eat, and your doctor who ensures good health to digest the food.

Abraham Lincoln (Goodwin 2006) always considered his stake-holders. As he won the U.S. Presidency, he had many enemies who didn't see his capabilities or agree with his politics or mindset. In any case, he recognized the intellect and value of many of these rivals and appointed them to official positions in his cabinet because they were the experts at what they did. These rivals eventually came to acknowledge and respect Lincoln for his political, humanistic, and brilliant approaches to governing. They found his brilliance through his perspectives, plans, and actions that led to success in bringing a divided country back together. He made stakeholders out of rivals because he needed them to work together and with him to achieve this result.

Stakeholders are always present, impactful, unavoidable, and essential to autonomous work. As autonomous workers, the 21st

> **How do you build stakeholdership with your colleagues?**

century requires that the right questions be asked and answered for good decision making. The people with the answers are all stakeholders to your endeavors. Without successful interactions with these people, autonomy cannot survive or thrive. And you cannot be effective in the 21st century without autonomy.

Establishing stakeholder needs for communication directs and enables the conversation. Having no insights into a stakeholder is often the reality of a situation. A set of conversation starters will help build a relationship of understanding and trust with the person with whom you are communicating (Brooks 2020). Humans need to be heard before they can listen to another perspective. These conversation starters facilitate that hearing and listening. Styles of communication and planning also facilitate good and effective communication. Refer to Chapter 2 "Defining Mindset Components" for a detailed description of nine conversation starters, such as conveying awe with a person's accomplishments, repeating the common goal of your connection, and/or facilitating a self-defined solution to an issue, as modes of work.

Stakeholders Versus Shareholders

The Business Roundtable, led by Jaime Dimon, Chairman and CEO of JPMorgan Chase, decided to change its purpose statement to focus on stakeholders versus shareholders. All 180 member companies agreed that stakeholders are more important in 21st century conditions than the singular focus on shareholders and making money for them. Stakeholders include employees and customers, as well as shareholders/owners. The companies' advocation was to give equal focus and attention to all three groups. This proclamation actually recognizes the need for stakeholder involvement in decision making.

How do you make stakeholders of those with whom you are not necessarily familiar? Striving to understand their goals, values, beliefs, and mode of work can help you predict and accommodate their behaviors and decisions. But first you need to identify all of the stakeholders who hold the power of supporting or derailing your work.

Stephen Covey (Covey 1989) urges people to seek to understand before being understood. This strategy gives you the advantage of knowing about another's needs prior to trying to fulfill them. Building stakeholdership with trust and relationship is based on another's needs being met.

Trust-building conversations and interactions can build understanding and a working relationship with stakeholders in an initiative. Building a profile for all of them can clarify stakeholder needs and, then, guide your work to fulfill them. The Wall Street Journal article, *So Many Stakeholders. How do Companies Choose Who to Satisfy?* (Taylor 2021) presents a realistic approach to actually being able to address the needs of all categories of your stakeholders, such as investors, customers, employees, suppliers, and communities. How do you meet all of these needs, especially when the needs are in conflict with each other, without making promises that cannot be fulfilled. Consider the risk of being labeled hypocritical with these promises, diminishing stakeholders' trust and relationship. Alison Taylor, author of the article, suggests a solution. The steps include:

1. Identify all stakeholder needs and their levels of relevance to a project.
2. Gather insights and suggestions from your internal teams on your analysis.
3. Prioritize these needs and relevance based on internal (your own) and external (stakeholders') priorities using four quadrants of an x and y axis.

A recent fundraising community for women with common goals and values has been very successful, increasing their contributions by enormous measures. The New York Times (Safronova 2021) reports that in previous times, women and contributions were presented in their husbands' names. Women today want their own identity as philanthropists and are changing their mode of fundraising and contributions to represent themselves and their interests. This focus has initiated a new model of stakeholdership in fundraising. These women stakeholders have formed a community that reinforces their needs and goals with a common understanding and platform for giving. They have created their own identity as philanthropists.

LinkedIn's Jeff Weiner (Weiner, Graduation Speech 2018) notes that compassion is the best characteristic that a new graduate can have. Understanding others, how they think, and how they will behave gives you an advantage in any and all circumstances of life. Weiner defines empathy and compassion to be different. Empathy, sensing another's pain, can make you just as helpless as the other person by also feeling that pain. Compassion allows you to recognize another's pain and be able to take action to stop the pain. Figure 6.2 shows a detailed stakeholder analysis.

Your goal, tasks, beliefs	Stakeholder and industry	Likely goals and beliefs
Goal: Certify employees as knowledge workers	1. Funder, Banking	1. Positive new revenue
Tasks: Build awareness of mindset	2. Buyer, Middle Market Technology CEOs	2. Worker self-sufficiency
	3. Employee, Technology	3. Control of own destiny
Beliefs: Everyone can build success	4. Partner, Education	4. Lifelong learning skills
	5. Supplier, Information Technology	5. User influence for design

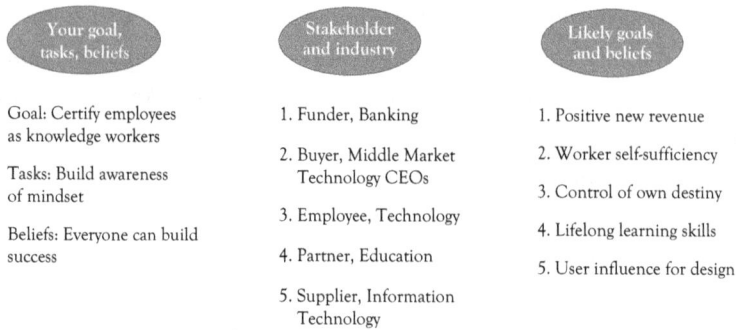

Figure 6.2 Stakeholder analysis

Building stakeholdership is based on compassion, understanding the needs, intent, and actions of another, and then taking action to relate. Weiner describes his own newly found compassion as he embraced it for leading a company. He focused on setting people up to succeed, rather than focusing on their mistakes and weaknesses.

Your stakeholders each hold a set of goals, values, beliefs, and mode of work. These mindset components provide great context for the success of your initiatives as you are dependent on them for your joint work. Stakeholders' mindsets have to align with project goals for collaboration to succeed.

Autonomy: Independent, Dependent, Interdependent

Autonomous work includes identifying work that needs to be done and who might be stakeholders in that work, as contributors or creating obstacles to your work and goals.

> *Lincoln, when competing for the Presidency, had his own ideas on how and what would earn him the position. He did not rely on his supporters to direct this endeavor but he did delegate the work to them to carry out his own design and plan. He focused on communicating his intent, his values, and what he had identified as the voters' intent and needs. He was autonomous in his independent approach with a dependence on the help of his stakeholders to implement his ideas.*

Autonomous work is independent while dependent. Although autonomous knowledge workers need to make decisions, the input to these decisions will most likely come from many sources. This makes a cycle of independent and dependent work, engaging those who are critical to your work and autonomy.

The way you work is often overlooked as an obstacle to achieving your goals. A small change in your expectations, being a value or belief modification, can have significant value in aligning work with others. If you believe that you are responsible for all outcomes of any collaboration and that your individual work is most important, then you are going to work in a mode that takes total responsibility for the outcome, blinding yourself to your dependency on contributions and progress made by others as stakeholders. Your metric for success and mode of work will validate your work alone. This notion of total responsibility will lead to disaster because of the undeniable influence and impact of others and their work. This is a behavior that demonstrates a belief that there is nothing to gain from others and their work. It will have to change.

Building and Managing Stakeholdership With Trust and Relationship

Continuous attention to maintaining a trusting relationship is essential. Changes in the project, resources, stakeholder situations, and external conditions have to be considered. Managing these changes and challenges can be facilitated with the common goal and behaviors and decisions that support that goal. When there is visibility and awareness of the common thread guiding work, trust and relationship are reinforced. This requires continuous awareness, exploration, and communication of where and how that thread is apparent.

The discussion and recognition of the hierarchy of goals can demonstrate work toward the common goal to reinforce the trust and relationship already established for the project. Outcomes are recognized as they fit into the flow of work within the hierarchy of goals. If there is no fit, there is reason for exploration into possible pivoting to realign work and stakeholdership.

Evaluating trust and relationship on a regular basis also enables adjustments to work to support the project. It is also valuable to continuously identify new stakeholders as new dimensions of the project evolve. Their mindset needs can interfere with established trust and relationship and, therefore, with achieving the goals of the project. Maintained trust and relationship act as insurance for meeting project goals.

> *Lincoln never forgot his responsibility to the people. When campaigning to be elected, he would humbly state that he truly wanted to represent the people and their needs but if they chose someone else for this role, he would respect that choice and not be disappointed at that time. He related to them his ability to keep trying and not give up due to a failure. He was committed to the people and their needs for freedom and self-sustainability.*

Checking Diligent Use of Protocols

Individual and organizational protocols often become relaxed as work evolves and becomes more comfortable. When relaxed, they can cause problems that are avoidable with stricter adherence. A comprehensive review of these protocols can be very useful in identifying the source of a problem. These protocols include:

- Awareness of vision/goals, mission/goals, values, beliefs, and mode of work
- Team work commitment and engagement of subject-matter expertise
- Agreement on hierarchy of goals, workplans, timelines, and expected outcomes
- Modes of work defined: time, deadlines, communication, workflow analysis, decision making, respect for subject-matter expertise
- Recognition and reward processes to continuously reinforce and align work

Do you create your individual and team protocols?

Communication stages can support and maintain these protocols, including attention to the readiness, relevance, reinforcement, and reflection on work activity. These stages are described in Chapter 9 "An Autonomous Environment."

Alignment: Tracking Progress

Setting goals is important but not as important as actually being able to reach your goals. Reaching your goals is a matter of awareness, mindset, resources, and persistence in pursuing them. Recognizing hierarchical, incremental progress and pivots can be done through systematic tracking of the results of your work. Consider tracking your goals, supporting mindsets, outcomes expected, actual outcomes, and pivots needed. Where do you see gaps? Using the archetype workflow analysis as previously mentioned can help find the cause of a gap or obstacle.

Ensuring Recognition and Rewards

Work that is recognized and rewarded continues. Remember that rewarding yourself and your stakeholders ensures that positive work will continue. Recognition can be informal and just referenced in conversation. Rewards are more formal and can happen on a regular schedule.

A system of recognition and rewards is most important in an autonomous environment. Knowledge workers have to evaluate their work continuously, so the feedback of others is very helpful.

Artifacts That Suggest a Mode of Work: Your Narrative Story

The artifacts of your mode of work, including your behaviors and decisions, create your narrative. These artifacts include:

- Autonomy
  - Ability to work with others, meet them where they are with mindset awareness
  - Mindset to seek a result
  - Confidence in stated work
  - Open to compromise with short-term gains leading to longer-term results
  - Compassion for differing mindsets, compromise for small wins
  - Trust and relationship building, using conversation starters
- Continuous checking your narrative with mindset and outcomes to manage it

- Concern for others' perspectives
- Frequent inquiry, listening, openness to new ideas, and planning
- Humility and honesty in evaluating your behaviors and decisions
- Being persistent
- Use of data and information to support inquiry and decison making

These characteristics are clues to how your mindset drives behaviors and decisions. These are essential elements for knowing how to work with others for alignment and success.

Worksheet Reference

Worksheets to facilitate using the concepts in this chapter are found in "Developing the Intentional Mindset, Module 4: Setting Beliefs and Modes of Work." The worksheets include:

Understanding Beliefs
Recognizing Mode of Work
Theory X. Y, Z for Leaders
Resource Allocation and Budgeting for Knowledge Work for Leaders
Members' Satisfiers and Motivators for Leaders
Mentor and Mentee Support
Decision making and Communication Protocols and Guidelines
Organizational Goals, Metrics, and Measures for Leaders
Brainstorming, Brainsteering, and Mind Mapping Processes
Team Charter Template
Readiness, Relevance, Reinforcement, and Reflection Communications
Idealized Design for Future Needs

Call to Action

Consider how you can best build awareness of your mindset components on a regular basis:

1. Define your goals, values, beliefs, and mode of work.
2. Define the triggers that spark your goals, values, beliefs, and mode of work.

3. Define your mindset when you had your best success and when you had a failure. How might you build continuous attention to your mindset to best serve your destiny?

4. What are the mindset components you would like to always serve you? What components can you consider changing as your work or scenarios changes? Goals, values, beliefs, or mode of work? How will you know when you need to change them?

5. Plan a schedule for regular review of your mindset components for modification, if needed.

Chapter Summary

This chapter connects your beliefs (biases) and mode of work to your goals and values. It also aligns these mindset components to those of your stakeholders and organization. The next chapter presents a description of a learning system that facilitates the use of mindset to master autonomous decision-making work in the knowledge economy.

SECTION III

Using a Learning System

CHAPTER 7

Ensuring Inquiry With a Learning System

A technology company realized that its customers needed training on the use of their complex software products. A training program was created but, after several months, customers seemed to need some additional support. Even though the program was designed and structured for consistency and high quality, the

In the autonomous 21st century environment, systematic inquiry and decisions drive destiny. Data and information improve the quality of those decisions and the right questions drive relevant data and information collection.

training program seemed to fall short of customer needs since some customers had to use the software but others had to maintain its connectivity throughout the company. The education expert assessed the problem. It seemed that there were two audiences for the training so a second program had to be created for the software engineers who had to maintain the software as it integrated into company operations. The specific needs were assessed and two courses were created to complement each other and to accommodate both audiences. The customers were happier and software satisfaction grew. A new narrative of effectiveness and service was created for the software company. Inquiry and research directed the program development and new narrative for effectiveness. Sales of the training doubled twice, once because of the second training program and secondly due to the enthusiasm of the customers.

Inquiry and learning enable you to sustain yourself and your organization. Nothing stands still, change is constant, and those who can accommodate the change with inquiry and learning are the winners in today's 21st century knowledge economy.

Do you ever feel overwhelmed with a task? Have no idea where to start, but would really like to be successful in finding a solution? The art of inquiry and learning make decision making and achievement routine and less complex. Consistent consideration of problems, opportunities, feasibility, and mindset needs of all stakeholders will guide you toward best outcomes. A learning system guides inquiry and relevant data collection so that all of your work and activities are advised by learning that helps you manage toward desired outcomes.

Consider the learning mindset (Dweck 2016). Your ambition to solve a problem or know something new is about learning and evaluation. Are you interested in knowing more or are you satisfied with what you already know when solving a problem or making a decision? The most maximized mindsets are those of learners as opposed to status quo confirmers. No matter the issue, problem, or scenario at hand, learners continuously seek clarity and options for solutions that enable the best decision possible for a sustainable outcome. In the knowledge economy, growth is often the desired outcome. Confirmers, who seek the status quo, are held back by their current beliefs. When challenges or discrepancies happen, confirmers resort to what they already know, sometimes called heuristics. Learners want to know more about the conditions/triggers that created a situation and, more importantly, consider options for solving the dilemma in a positive and growth-oriented manner. Even when you decide that the status quo is the best option, that decision should be based on learning to validate that approach.

Data and information help you to understand conditions, your own mindset, and the mindsets of your stakeholders. This allows you to speculate on a next round of inquiry, suggest possible solutions, collect more data and information, and, ultimately, make decisions that are more strategically focused. Managing your decision drivers can lead to different and better results. Thinking ahead and/or thinking again allows you to reconsider a situation from differing perspectives and enables better decisions.

> **Do you always consider relevant data and information when making a decision?**

Dylan Baird (Baird 2022) founded Philly Foodworks in 2014. After college, he worked for an urban farm and became disillusioned with farming's lack of ability to sustain itself. It seems that farmers were dependent upon grants, and so on, to keep them in business. Baird's vision was one of creating positive social impact. The funders were not so interested in social impact, but in other areas based on their goals. If his great social impact idea for farming was not to be funded but a lesser idea was funded based on the desires and interest of the funder, Baird decided to pursue his own vision and started his own farming initiative with no dependency on anyone but himself and a team he would assemble to help him.

Baird was not trained in farming strategy or techniques. His interests were more in the people, marketing, and problem-solving arena. He knew of people's need for and interest in local farm products, healthy food alternatives, and about the local varieties available. He also knew of the difficulties that farmers had with meeting these needs and interests. Once the farming was done for the day, the farmer had to attend to the business aspects of selling, distributing products, and the financial margins to sustain themselves. Community Supporting Associations (CSAs) were helpful but provided little flexibility for local families because the subscription model of weekly deliveries was not flexible. It was not possible to request certain products when needed, as there was a standard delivery every week. There was also the farmers' issue of retaining customers since buying was not consistent.

Baird was determined to strategize on how to evaluate all of these components and come up with a model to serve both the farmers and the local families in need of local produce. A significant contribution to this solution was the software that Baird and his team acquired in 2016. This tool automated orders, modifications, distribution routes, packaging amounts, scheduling, and customer requests. He went into the business of automated delivery management.

The key ideas in this chapter include:

- Defining the learning system
- Implementing the learning system
- Maximizing queries and analysis
- Digital nervous system to support the learning system

Defining the Learning System

Having a learning mindset allows you to structure inquiries for systematic data collection and evaluation that lead to better decisions and better des-

Is learning a part of every-thing you do?

tiny. Relevant questions, relevant data, and the learning gained are key to the decision-making process. Using a learning system ensures that strategic inquiry, data, and decisions routinely lead to your best outcomes. The impact of a learning system is undeniably effective in managing your work.

Learning systems have three unique purposes:

- To establish the value of learning as part of your mindset and organizational practices
- To add learning considerations, especially mindset analysis, to all decisions
- To add inquiry and learning context to data collection leading to relevant decisions

Each of the six learning system steps requires inquiries and data collection to move through your initiative for best outcomes at each step. The six learning system steps and inquiries include:

1. *Mindset Awareness*: Understanding and evaluating mindsets—your own, organization, stakeholders, and the project needs
   - What are your mindset components: goals, values, beliefs, and mode of work?
   - What are your organization's, project's, and stakeholders' mindsets?
   - What mindset is needed to implement your initiative?
   - What mindsets will lessen or improve your outcome?
   Baird had a desire to form a business that was true to his own vision of making a positive difference for urban families and to be self-sustaining in that endeavor. He needed to understand the mindset of the farmers and that of the local families who would benefit from fresh,

local farm produce. He also understood the needs of the distributors who were trying to effectively connect the farmers to the families. His solution would have to serve all stakeholders.

2. ***Entrepreneurial/Intrapreneurial Options:*** Finding solutions, options, or opportunities that will solve a problem or create new value

   - What do you wish to solve or create?
   - What are the conditions that shape your initiative?
   - What options or opportunities are available to assist in solving an issue or creating new value?
   - What mindset is needed for each of these options to succeed?

     Philly Foodworks had significant challenges to sustain itself as a self-sufficient entity. Baird looked at the issues of all of his stakeholders in order to design a solution in service to himself and to all others, especially the farmers and the families who wanted healthy, local produce. He explored other, similar providers to confirm that his challenges were universal. He explored the reasons for lack of customer retention that seemed to be caused by inconsistent purchasing. He calculated all costs of logistics, timing of delivery, and transportation overhead. He researched possible ways to bring all of these costs down and support all stakeholders in the food industry in their ability to survive and thrive. He modified his mindset from that of a farmer to that of a back-end business coordinator for farmers and their local families. This made costs lower, services more consistent, and retention higher.

3. ***Economic Analysis:*** Quantifying options with economic analysis, testing the feasibility

   - What product or service defines a selected option?
   - What is the supply and demand for that option?
   - What are the production possibilities for that option?
   - What are the opportunity costs of that option?
   - What are the impactful externalities of that option?

     Philly Foodworks couldn't exist as a direct distributor from local farmers to urban families. Business margins were not sustainable, so Baird decided to focus on the supply side of his operations. Who were his stakeholders and who could he help with his new software capability? What were those capabilities that he had developed over the last few years to accommodate his growing demand as well as the logistical needs to expand his delivery services? What was the economic benefit of these software capabilities that could be shared with others? Better prices for farmers and less driving for distributors resulted in lower prices for urban families, making a good economic scenario for all.

4. ***Emotional/Mindset Analysis:*** Qualifying options with mindset analysis, testing the acceptance of all stakeholders
   - What are the mindsets of all stakeholders regarding the selected option?
   - How do these mindsets align with the mindset needed for the option to be successful?
   - What is the gap in mindset?
   - What would fill that mindset gap for success?

   Baird, being a people-focused person, was aware of the value of local farming to urban families. He also understood the farmers' mindsets that maintained their interest and passion for farming. As a business person, he saw the challenges for the distributors' services, as well. He designed a distributor services model using his software that made it feasible and attractive for farmers to continue to farm and urban families to count on timely and desired product deliveries. In the context of the 21st century emerging trend of online buying, he would expand his software to create an e-commerce site to manage distribution and ordering for farmers and for urban families. Central receiving hubs would streamline farmer deliveries and pick-up for urban families. Flexibility in ordering, based on the lower distributor costs, would be offered. All of these services would be managed through software automated data collection and guidance. Both stakeholders would benefit from Baird's model. Baird's own business would expand. Farmers' goals to farm and families' value in heathy, locally grown food were foundational to Baird's solution.

5. ***Implementation:*** Defining a project plan and work to implement the workflow of the selected option
   - What is the purpose and objective of the project?
   - What project plan steps need to be planned?
   - What are the milestones to be achieved in the hierarchy of goals?

- What resources are needed? Where and when are these resources available?
- How will workflow steps be checked for meeting milestones?
- What are the project protocols to streamline activity, communications, and decisions?
- What is the timeline for achieving each milestone?
- Where and when do outcomes not match expected results? What are the obstacles, mindset or otherwise? How can these obstacles be eliminated?

Baird had to plan his transition to a different business model based on all of the data and information he collected from his initial work as a distributor. His business and problem-solving tendencies made him aware of all aspects of his operations and all of the stakeholders' needs as they came about. Baird created a project for his staff to manage this transition and its continued effectiveness. As they worked through the project steps, they were continuously collecting data on expected and actual outcomes in order to plan pivots to make outcomes better. Keeping his original goal in mind of pursuing positive social impact and being self-sustaining, he defined and initiated projects to achieve these goals while tending his stakeholders and customers.

Once stakeholders engaged in his solutions, he had to implement them by building an organization to accommodate growing needs. He had to plan hiring, infrastructure to guide work autonomously, create a team to manage everyone's work, and continue his own work of seeking and reviewing new growth opportunities as they aligned with his vision and his business model.

6. **Reflection**: Considering actual versus expected outcomes for pivoting as needed, identifying the benefits and impact of work completed, becoming aware of new opportunities
   - What work met expected outcomes as opposed to actual outcomes?
   - What obstacles intervened to create this gap?
   - How can these obstacles be removed or modified to enable the expected outcomes? Do the expected outcomes need to be modified?
   - What impact did any and all outcomes create?

- What impact suggests current or future value to be created?

In 2018, Baird realized that he and his team were openly pursuing any/all seemingly related opportunities to the detriment of his focus on the core business of his e-commerce site and his secondary focus of paying down his current debt. This realization led Baird to streamline his efforts and considerations to advancing his core business only and to pay down his debt. This was a very lucky decision because of the increased demand due to the pandemic virus and the curtailment of people's mobility. Philly Foodworks business grew from 500 deliveries per week to 500 deliveries per day. How would the company manage this increase? They would have to scale their systems to accommodate more orders and expand the staff from 11 to 60 members. Internal infrastructure and communications would have to be designed to grow accordingly. This suggested several new projects to be defined and implemented.

Baird also recognized that his mode of work would have to change. With such an expansion, his team of nine managers would have to make operational decisions, determine changes to processes, define compensation for new employees, and design software modifications, as needed, without his input. Baird would be left out of these decisions as he was busy with strategic business concerns and growth. He had to reconcile himself to the notion that others' decision making was not intended to leave him out. His team members were consulting each other regarding decisions and were just being efficient as knowledge workers. He had to see the decisions as business routines and not as personal issues. In reflecting on the autonomous environment of decision making that he had set up, Baird made that reconciliation.

Data and information collection for reflecting on each of these inquiries is essential and customized to individual work. It is not general, but specific to the circumstances and stakeholders of the work. Backtracking through the six steps is often needed when obstacles occur and reconsideration of a previous step is necessary. The purpose of this step is to improve an outcome or create new value. Refer to Chapter 8

"Reflections, New Value, and Celebrations" for a detailed analysis of the reflection process.

Implementing the Learning System

A learning system integrates all work to make each step productive in reaching a desired outcome (Ariely 2010; Drucker 1985; MacMillan and McGrath 2000; Schumpeter 1934; Senge 1990; Thaler and Sunstein 2009). The learning system steps provide an incremental system of inquiry and analysis to plan and integrate work that will meet economic and stakeholders' expectations. A learning system overview follows. Each learning system step has an expected outcome. This expected outcome guides the queries and data and information collection that will define your work. Table 7.1 describes the work of the learning system.

> **How do you use your learning? How does it lead to a decision?**

Maximizing Queries and Analysis

Learning system steps are dependent on the right queries to guide data and information collection and analyses. Various queries and their characteristics are described in the following.

Queries

The knowledge pyramid provides a very simple description of how you, as a knowledge worker, can streamline your research to achieve meaningful results. Data, the broadest category, is collected to cover everything related to a query. It is turned into information with an analysis of its relevance to the current environment and needs. Then the information is analyzed to further distill it into knowledge that can be helpful to the current project. Finally, knowledge is used to create an action plan for project work. Figure 7.1 connects the knowledge pyramid to the six learning system steps that require data and information collection.

Table 7.1 Implementing the learning system steps

Learning System Steps	Defining Work	Expected Outcomes	Queries, Data and Information Collected
Mindset Awareness: Understanding and evaluating mindset—your own, organization, stakeholders, and the project needs	Define issue, objective, or opportunity	Clarity of purpose	What is the problem, need, or opportunity?
	Desired results with timeframe	Clarity of impact, expected result, and timing	What is the gap that needs to be filled and when?
	Current state	Current state of issue or need	What caused the problem or need?
	Mindset needed for decision making (goal, values, beliefs, and mode of work)	Mindset profile definition	What mindset qualities are needed to pursue a solution to fill the gap between the current state and the desired state?
Entrepreneurial Options: Finding solutions, options, or opportunities that will solve a problem or create new value	Explore solution options with stakeholders involved	List of potential options for solution or value creating	What are the Drucker 7 options for new value? (See Chapter 8 "Reflections, New Value, and Celebrations")
		Customers and stakeholders impacted	Who are customers for each other? Stakeholders for each option?
			What are their mindset needs and how would they be impacted by each option?
Economic Analysis: Quantifying options with economic analysis, testing for feasibility	Consider economic factors related to project goals	Project goals with metrics and measures	What does the project need to achieve?
			What metric and measures will determine its success?
		Range of possible goal fulfillment	What are the minimum and maximum goal parameters?
		Economic factors to consider	What is the supply and demand for a selected option?
			What are the production possibilities?
			What are the opportunity costs?
			What are the externalities?
		Changes needed to the goal based on economic feasibility?	What change in the goal might be needed to fit into the parameter range?

		Stakeholders and their mindsets	Who impacts and/or is impacted by this project, its goal, and work? Their mindset needs?
Emotional Analysis: Qualifying options with mindset analysis, testing acceptance of all stakeholders	Consider current stakeholder mindsets and align with project mindset needed for decision making	Option/project mindset needed	What are mindset needs of the option/project?
		Mindset alignment needs	How do stakeholder mindsets and project mindsets align?
			What change needs to occur for the alignment of mindsets?
Implementation: Defining a project plan and work to implement the workflow of the selected option	Purpose of selected option	Project objective and outcome	What is the purpose of this project?
			What is the outcome expected?
	Create a workplan with tasks, stakeholder results, decision making, expected outcomes, and milestones	Workplan with milestones, metrics, deliverables, timelines	How is work to be completed in workplan steps?
			How and when will work be measured based on what metric?
	Test for expected outcomes with workflow archetype analysis; align work and mindsets as needed for decision making using decisions influencers and choice architectures	Workplan predictions of inputs and outputs with metrics and milestones anticipated	What is the outcome for each workplan step?
			What are the inputs to each workplan step?
		Adjustments to accommodate missed outcomes	What are the milestones, metrics, and measures to be achieved within each step of the workplan?
			How and what adjustments will resolve missed outcomes?
	Evaluate and acquire resources as needed	Resource plan with needs, availability, and plan to acquire if needed	What resources are needed to complete workplan steps?
			What is their availability?
			How will you acquire those not available?
	Set up operational protocols of project charter, timeline, communications, metrics, measures	Project charter, including stakeholders, milestones, metrics, measures, timelines, decision making and communication protocols, and resources needed	What is the mode of work for this project, including stakeholders and their modes of work?
			How will team members communicate?
			How will decisions be made?
			How will resources be added into the project work?

(Continued)

Table 7.1 (Continued)

Learning System Steps	Defining Work	Expected Outcomes	Queries, Data and Information Collected
	Implement a continuous review routine to identify missed outcomes and pivots needed	Shared journaling, weekly status updates, pivots defined	What needs to be reported regularly?
			Who needs to be accountable for reporting?
			What are the components and format of this report?
			How are pivots evaluated and implemented?
	Schedule recognition and reward routine to celebrate outcomes, mindset alignment, and achievement	Recorded recognition and rewards protocol, shared for all to review, including detailed deliverables, mindset work, and alignment	What are the criteria for recognition and rewards?
			What are the formats for delivering them?
			How and when are they tracked and scheduled?
			How are recognition and reward needs evaluated?
Reflection: Considering actual versus expected outcomes for pivoting as needed, identifying the benefits and impact of work completed, becoming aware of new opportunities	Reflect on all work for evaluation of efficiency and/or effectiveness to improve outcomes	Journal of reflections	What is the format and timing of journal entries?
			How is the journal shared?
			What are the expectations for journal use?
	Identify and review operational systems and their integration for improving outcomes	Pivots needed and implemented	How does an action happen when suggested in the journal?
	Review work in the context of global, regional, and local trends and events, unexpected outcomes, and so on		How is this action measured?
		New value opportunities due to integration of operational systems	How are other ideas and opportunities shared for evaluation?
		Global and other trends and events that could positively or negatively impact current activities	What are the economic and mindset needs of each idea or opportunity?
			How can operations be combined to improve efficiency and effectiveness?

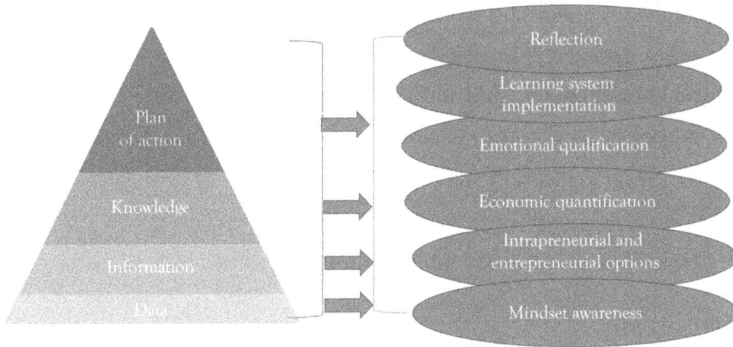

Figure 7.1 *Learning system framework for data and information collection*

This path of analysis and thinking is also supported by Benjamin Bloom's taxonomy of seven levels of inquiry. Refer to Chapter 2 "Defining Mindset Components." These levels structure the research process to build relevance and deep understanding of a specific scenario.

Forming Research Inquiries: Five Whys and Seven Levels of Thinking

The *Five Whys* method of inquiry is a simple tool to identify the biases and/or reasons that can cloud objective consideration of a problem. Why did you make a specific decision? Why did you believe that? Why did you have a bias toward that belief? Why did you value that action? What are the other biases that impacted your actions or research?

The *Five Whys* approach guides your data and information collection and analysis for each learning system step. Your mindset, problem, and economic and emotional needs are validated with *Five Whys* inquiry.

> *In building his business, Baird did not act on instinct or bias, he acted on the data he retrieved from actual revenue accounting and stakeholder feedback that described actual logistics, transportation, orders, and their consistency. Baird also surveyed for stakeholder economic and emotional needs to be met.*

The *Five Whys* approach to inquiry can be combined with the seven levels of thinking taxonomy. Bloom's seven levels of inquiry and thinking are useful to sequentially shape your collection, analysis, and evaluation of relevant data and information.

The knowledge pyramid includes the following sequence of data analyses, supported by Bloom's taxonomy of inquiry for thinking and learning.

Data

Facts : Build awareness and identification of basic facts and concepts.

Information

Understanding: Explain why facts and/or concepts are important or relevant, including characteristics and connections between/among the facts and concepts.

Application: Use facts and/or concepts as they apply to new situations.

Knowledge

Analysis: Differentiate facts and concepts to identify individual impact.

Synthesis: Consider facts and concepts together as they might create a new and interdependent system to create new value.

Action Plan

Evaluation: Use economic and emotional analyses to justify the costs, benefits, and value of any new idea.

Create: Produce new and original work or value through design and development.

This structure is very helpful in guiding inquiry, relevant data and information research, and, ultimately, learning. Figure 7.2 describes how these two tools complement each other to facilitate relevant inquiry.

Bloom's Inquiry and Five Whys Analyses

- **Knowledge**—Recall facts and basic concepts. Why are these facts? Why do they support basic concepts?

Figure 7.2 (Continued)

- **Understanding**—Why facts and concepts are relevant? Why are characteristics supportive? Why are connections made? Why are they relevant? Why are they not relevant?
- **Application**—Why do facts and concepts apply to new situations? Why are they helpful? Why is that help meaningful? Why is that meaningfulness valuable? Why will others value it?
- **Analysis**—Why are facts meaningful? Why do they convey concepts? Why are concepts meaningful? Why do facts and concepts complement each other? Why do they provide separate value?
- **Synthesis**—Why do facts and concepts together create new value? Why does that new value matter? Why might that new value conflict with other activities? Why does this new value align with stakeholders' needs? Why does the new value contribute to stakeholders' needs?
- **Evaluation**—Why do the facts and concepts create costs? Why is their new value balancing with those costs? Why might the new value create external and extra costs? Why might a consideration of overlaps be important? Why do gaps and overlaps create costs as opposed to benefits?
- **Create**—Why do facts and concepts benefit the design of new value? Why do they contribute to the assembly of new value? Why do they contribute to the audience for the new value? Why do they impact growth potential? Why might the new value lead to other opportunities?

Figure 7.2 Five Whys facilitating Bloom's seven levels of inquiry

Workflow and Archetype Analysis

Workflow and archetypes forecast how systems work within an organization. These generic formulas allow you to observe the flow of work and outcome at each step to understand why and where archetype obstacles may be causing conflicts. This analysis helps define inquiry and data collection for new insights into the obstacles and how to eliminate them.

There are 10 classic archetype models to consider when analyzing a workflow and its outcomes. They are useful for seeing work patterns and planning how to manage work for the results you are expecting. Sometimes an adjustment in outcome expectations could be warranted. Also, an unexpected outcome could lead to an unexpected opportunity. These 10 workflow archetypes include:

1. **Limits to growth:** Accelerating growth is limited due to internal or external response, such as resource constraints or saturation levels leading to negative reactions.

2. **Shifting the burden:** Short-term solution lessens the effort toward fundamental long-term corrective measures.

3. **Shifting the burden with intervenor:** Same as above, but further ameliorates the problem as system members never learn to deal with the problem themselves.

4. **Balancing process with delay:** Too much corrective action in response to a delay builds no awareness of progress being made.

5. **Eroding goals:** Short-term solution lets long-term, fundamental goals decline.

6. **Escalation:** System members or organizations see themselves dependent on building advantage over each other; threatened members escalate their work and offerings to the point of unrealistic outcomes.

7. **Success to the successful:** As activities compete for limited resources, successful activities are given more resources than the others, leading to their further success.

8. **Tragedy of the commons:** Use of commonly available but limited resources solely for individual use restricts others' use of those resources.

9. **Fixes that fail:** A short-term fix has unforeseen long-term consequences that may require more of the short-term fix.

10. **Growth underinvestment:** Growth is limited by underinvestment in additional resources as growth reaches its capacity.

Mindset Biases

Mindset determines what questions you ask, which dictates what you find. Your mindset biases impact the queries and, therefore, the results of the research. Your research becomes selective and not objective in its considerations and conclusions. If you value collaboration, then queries to solve a problem will include multiple perspectives. If your goal is to be seen as correct by others, then queries will only seek support for your initial evaluation of the situation.

Awareness of the ubiquity of bias can be very helpful in identifying it and minimizing its impact. A strong inclination toward data-driven and evidenced-based decision making will weaken these biases (Lomangino 2015).

Decisions and data collection are dependent on the right and relevant questions. Beliefs or biases can be neutralized with careful

> **Do you check for a bias when structuring your learning queries?**

thinking through the levels of Bloom's taxonomy. Levels of knowledge, understanding, and application should identify factual data and information and eliminate assumptions and opinions. Levels of analysis, synthesis, evaluating, and creating identify options for defining value-creating outcomes. Within the learning system, these levels of inquiry help you explore the realms of opportunity, economic feasibility, and emotional/mindset that are essential to making good decisions.

When working in a farming organization, Baird was able to identify a bias in the values of external funders that did not match his own thinking and values. He eliminated the impact of that external bias by pursuing his own farming operation that was aligned to his own value for social impact. He could see others' needs and wanted to help them with their challenges. When he realized that he had a tool that could be used to meet the needs of his stakeholders, he did not try to make gains for himself only. He adapted the software tool to be of use to others, thus reinforcing his ultimate vision of positive social impact. On the contrary, Baird could have kept his software to himself and focused solely on his own successes. His belief in the value of people influenced his business research and decisions.

When Mindsets and Decisions Don't Match

Mindsets lead to decisions and when conflict arises, mindsets can be altered to circumvent the conflict. There are two tools to help with these alternations:

- **Decision influencers**—Influencing decisions, both your own and those of your stakeholders, using related and relevant data and information, helps people by sharing a new context of a situation (Thaler 2016). Related and relevant data and information can provide a new and different perspective to a problem that can influence thinking and decisions with perspectives that have not been previously considered.
- **Choice architectures**—Choices with consequential results bring new insight into a decision. These choices broaden the understanding of the impact of a decision and, consequently, facilitate a better decision. Sometimes a choice architecture will make the better choice obvious and sometimes it is just a catalyst for deciding.

In the case of an obstacle identified in an archetype/workflow analysis, related data and information can help a knowledge worker alter a behavior or decision to eliminate the obstacle. Decision influencers and choice architectures are designed to accommodate the exact nature of the obstacle, the mindset cause, and its source. These tools are very powerful in helping manage mindsets that may not be matching for best decisions and results. Figure 7.3 describes an example of archetype analysis, decision influencer, and choice architecture.

Workflow: Masks to limit infections: avoidance of masks; high infections
- Short-term solution mindset: denial of my rights, uncomfortable, a nuisance; entitlement belief

Decision influencers/choice architectures:
- Decision influencers—data and information on infection rates with/without masks leading to rates of covid 19 control, impact to families' infections, impact of loss of income, balance of freedom with well-being on a value scale

- Choice architecture—likely infection or not, penalty for noncompliance

Figure 7.3 Archetypes, decision influencers, and choice architectures

Listening, explaining, showing respect for diverse values and beliefs while presenting other evidence that is contrary to the current thinking can alter a person's perspective. Posth (Posth 2008) continuously reminded his Chinese partners of the essence of the common goal

How do you resolve conflicts in mindsets?

and his commitment to them. His approach to conflict influenced stakeholders to shape new perspectives and eliminate the obstacle of their current thinking.

Digital Nervous System to Support the Learning System

Organizations need data and information described as a digital nervous system (Gates 1999) to support good decision making. Intrapreneuring and entrepreneuring require meaningful data and information for research. Data and information on external events and trends, as well as on current work and operations, should be included in this digital nervous system. Sources of trend, event, and customer data and information include news and journal articles, census, government agency databases, customer, survey data, and opinion pieces. Sources on current work include reflections and analysis on actual and expected outcomes, operational data and information, organizational members' profiling, and organizational member journaling. Digital availability of data and information often prompts creative thinking and the new opportunities it might uncover.

Knowledge workers will look for opportunities to create new value more readily when there are data and information to support those efforts. Basic inquiry on operations can be supported by data on sales, workflow, customers, and outcomes. These insights lead to possible changes that will improve operational outcomes, as well as introduce potential opportunities. Individual profiles can uncover skills, interests, and passions of members that can lead to new ideas or projects. Also, restructuring and filtering data and information through data mining techniques and regression analyses allow even further clarification on actual results, causes, and correlations that provide insights for the best management of outcomes and opportunities.

> **Do you have a personal digital nervous system?**

There are almost unlimited opportunities to collect and correlate data and information to serve an individual or organization. These methods should be customized to a specific workflow of operations, customer engagement, external trend, industry activity, and market opportunities. These data and information can also provide insight into decision rationale, allowing you to influence the mindset(s) that lead to those decisions.

Data Collection

All inquiries that are completed in the context of a learning system exponentially increase the potential for success. Data should always be relevant to the issue and current work (Davenport and Kim 2018). It can serve various purposes as follows:

- **Descriptive:** Statistics to support a point, text mining for new information to:
  - Understand the past.
  - Gather your own new data through experiments, surveys, and so on.
  - Assess the quality of data collected: yours and others.
  - Identify causation or correlation.
- **Predictive:** Data mining, forecasting, regression analysis, time series analysis:
  - Define the right metrics to be meaningful for guiding work.
  - Predict the future.
  - Define trends to be most likely and/or significant.
- **Prescriptive:** Optimization, experimental design:
  - Guide work and decision making with a desired result.
  - Presume to define a remedy to an issue.
  - Be persuasive.

When using the learning system, you can choose among these data possibilities depending on the inquiry you are researching.

Examples of Digital Nervous System Resources

Digital system resources will be different for every individual and organization. However, here is a start at identifying some common elements for consideration:

- **Customer data and information:** who, why, when, and where regarding current customers, their activity, and their mindsets
- **Sales data and information:** final and potential sales activity, progressive stages and journaling of sales activity
- **Operations measures and metrics:** goals planned, measures to track progress toward the targeted metric, noting performance for all operational areas
- **Market and competitor data and information:** current market events, activity, and trends, competitor events, activity, and trends
- **Global and industry data and information, and so on:** global events, activity, and trends, relevant census insights, and government databases
- **Industry standards for performance:** relevant certifications, areas and level of performance required, and holders of certifications
- **Competitor and stakeholder profiles and mindsets:** provides contextual data and information on competitors and stakeholders
- **Employee profiles:** provides contextual data and information on organizational members, including strengths, interests, experiences, and mindsets with goals
- **Company stories:** successes and failures, journal of interactions, and reflections and learnings on successes and failures
- **Recognition and rewards history:** journal of who, when, where, and for what recognition and reward has been conveyed
- **Budgetary context for research and intrapreneuring:** specific projects, financial amount allocated, expected return on investment, and available resources for new development

- **Protocols and parameters for operations and decisions:** defined processes and decision parameters to guide autonomous mode of work for all operational areas and practices
- **Organization vision, mission, and goals:** background information on all components of the organizational mindset, examples of vision and mission-oriented work
- **Project histories and status:** project descriptions and reflections on outcomes, successes, and failures on previous work and stakeholders
- **Learning system templates and project workplans:** templates to guide learning and project work using the learning system approach
- **Any other relevant data and information:** customized to a specific organization

The learning system requires that workers know how to use data and information to create knowledge for decision making. This knowledge will drive mindset awareness, entrepreneurial, economic, and mindset/emotional evaluations and decisions. Knowledge workers will learn to build context around all components of a task for better insights. Facts are separated from opinions through data analysis. The *Five Whys* used in the context of Bloom's taxonomy of thinking levels helps focus inquiries for increasingly deeper understanding and exploration of a situation or problem.

> *The catalyst to Philly Foodworks success has been the thoughtful and efficient use of data and information. It was collected as a routine during operations and recognized for its value as Baird systematically worked through the learning system steps to build self-sustainability and positive social impact into his company.*

Data and information are merely tools, the real intent and relevant use of them is found through the entrepreneurial, economic, and mindset/emotional analyses. This intentional and relevant use of data, information, and knowledge can be done only by a human being as enabled through a learning mindset. Technology, data, and information do not make decisions. They can only assist in clarifying factual conditions for making good decisions toward a goal to be met. Most important is the recognition that different analyses will occur depending on the mindset of the worker. A conclusion is not definitive, it is based on the context within which it was researched.

Worksheet Reference

Worksheets to facilitate using the concepts in this chapter are found in "Developing the Intentional Mindset, Module 5: Using a Learning System." The worksheets include:

Learning System Steps
Project Steps
Five Whys Analysis
Designing and Building the Digital Nervous System
Bloom's Taxonomy
Archetype/Workflow Analysis
Decision Influencers
Choice Architectures

Call to Action

Consider a recent project. Review the steps you took to complete this project as you refer to the six steps of the learning system.

1. Which steps did you do well?
2. Which steps could you have done with more energy and intentional effort?
3. Do you think you could have created more insight for yourself and others by more focus on any one of the six steps of the learning system?
4. How would you customize the learning system for your individual needs?

Chapter Summary

This chapter describes the learning system that enables autonomy and decision making for the 21st century knowledge economy work. The next chapter describes a comprehensive approach to reflecting on current and previous work and characteristics that can lead to new value creation.

CHAPTER 8

Reflections, New Value, and Celebrations

An established financial services company helped individual investors create investment plans to ensure a comfortable and well-funded retirement.

> **Reflecting is an essential practice of continuous learning and creating new value.**

The strategy was not necessarily seeking huge amounts of profit and growth, but more practically focused on the mindset of each investor as to desired lifestyle and security in old age. This approach suggested continued reflection and exploration of the needs of the anticipated life ahead. What did an individual foresee for life after retirement? What are the current pleasures that she would like to continue? What would these interests require in terms of funding? Reflecting was at the core of this investment approach, striving to accommodate the mindsets of the clients as each planned for a desired quality of life when work ended.

Socrates said that the "unexamined life is not worth living." Living without reflection? When you think about what has transpired, you are supporting yourself by collecting real-time data. There are two ways that this data can be very helpful: providing insights for improvements of current outcomes and prompting ideas for the future and new opportunities. These data collections can be systematically planned and structured to ensure insights and ideas. But how do you motivate yourself or others to actually delve into that thinking. Many people are convinced that they are *right* in their thinking and become defensive when you ask them probing questions. Structured reflection can strip away delusions and confirmation thinking that distort reality. It can offer invaluable hindsight, as well as forward-thinking perspectives.

Pope John XXIII (Gardner 1995) was thought of as a genial uncle to all, as opposed to the narrative of Pope Pius XII, his predecessor, as strict and unyielding in matters of Church doctrine and tradition. John was considered the universal shepherd of 900 million Catholics, ready to build modernistic approaches into traditional doctrines. His built this narrative over many years.

Pope John XXIII initiated the Second Vatican Council using his narrative as a compassionate leader with the purpose of aligning change with traditional doctrines of the Church. He sought open discussion and respectful debate on matters of conflicting perspectives. The Council engaged commissions to discuss and reflect on issues with opposing opinions and to use the findings of the commissions to make newly advised policies. He placed equal importance on the discussion process and on the content of the discussion. All perspectives were to be considered and accommodated. His commission topics stressed equality and the simple teaching of Christ. This approach represented the artifacts of his personal leadership narrative to consider all perspectives and to align through insightful reflection.

Do you intentionally trigger a reflection for every activity and decision?

Reflection is valuable when it happens *in the moment*. Considering actions, reactions, and their possible causes as they happen can lead to a change in perspective that can impact a result before it happens.

Key ideas in this chapter include:

- Background: defining new value
- Paths of reflection
- Celebrations

Let's explore how you can systematize these reflections for ensuring valuable insights that might lead to improvements in current scenarios. These insights might include:

- **Efficiency:** ways to reduce resources and energy used to achieve some aspect of work
- **Effectiveness:** opportunities to apply operational learning to individual systems to achieve a more streamlined workflow

Ideas for new opportunities include forward-thinking perspectives:

- **New integrations of workflow:** new synergies that can increase value through new offerings
- **Innovation in a new domain:** new ideas in related domains to create new products, new services, new customers, new partners/stakeholders, or a new industry or market

Background: Defining New Value

New value can be thought of as a driving and permanent goal for an organization. Change is constant and must be recognized and accommodated if an organization is to sustain itself even before it seeks to thrive with new value. Reflection paves the way to observing and maximizing the value that can be found in change. Several sources of change can be explored.

Idealizing Design

Ackoff, Magidson, and Addison (2008) developed a concept of idealized design. This concept includes forecasting future needs and trends and then building them into current thinking and planning. This thinking ensures that project work does not fall short of future needs as these needs evolve through the timeframe of the project itself.

Idealized design captures continuous changes in your environment that will impact current work and its outcomes. This approach actually systematizes change to create new value. Reflection on external but related activities brings awareness of these upcoming changes that need to be accommodated. Systematizing these future changes into your current work is essential in a competitive market or scenario.

Brainsteering and mind mapping will build new awareness through reflection. Work plans and agendas will accommodate this awareness of needs and biases as they occur.

Continuous Intrapreneuring

Knowledge workers are in control of their work and destinies, both their own and that of their organizations. Since change is constant, it makes sense that this knowledge worker control include continuous awareness of change and its potential. This is the art of intrapreneuring. Change creates interesting opportunities to consider new value. An autonomous environment within an organization can foster growth from within based on awareness and contemplation of change. This process is one of continuous learning through many types of reflection on environmental and global events and trends, customer insights, workflow/operational systems and strengths, and the possible integration of system components in new ways.

> Is the concept of new value always on your mind? For yourself and for others?

Awareness of your environment being global, regional, and local; a specific industry, market, customer; your employee strengths and interests; and of internal events can introduce new options and opportunities for growth. This awareness holds the key to improving productivity and performance. It allows knowledge workers to consider alternative paths to understand and improve current outcomes. These alternative paths might include evaluations of mindset, adjustment of goals and expected results, and possible pivots for better outcomes. This awareness also allows unexpected outcomes or trends to inspire new ideas and subsequent growth.

Amazon.com was founded in 1994 in Bellevue, Washington as an online seller of books. Jeffrey Bezos, its founder, envisioned the company as an ecommerce provider, not merely a seller of books. This vision led him to expand its online sales to include just about every-thing you need to live. The name Amazon was selected because of its reference to the vast South American river.

eBay was founded as ActionWeb to bring sellers and buyers together in an online market. It has evolved into a support infrastructure for those sellers, offering set-up services for sellers and connections that facilitate the buying and selling transactions. Founders were eager for expansive ideas on how to enhance their original concept.

Google was founded as an online search engine in 1997. It has now expanded to offer over 50 Internet services and products, includ-ing email, online document creation and management, and software for mobile phones and computers. Google expanded its original search capability to providing meaning to the endless data being accumu-lated and available on the Internet.

All of these expansions resulted from the ability to connect current products and services to future needs and opportunities.

Organization members can build their awareness to identify, quantify, and qualify options and opportunities according to a set of growth param-eters and services within their autonomous environment. Refer to Chap-ter 9 "Building an Autonomous Environment" for a detailed description of this environment. Intrapreneuring becomes a standard practice that is fostered by continuous and expected reflection.

Reflections for Growth Team

To systematize regular reflecting within an organization, a team can be useful. The Reflections for Growth (RFG) team will create a routine for reflecting and sharing thinking on improving current outcomes and new value opportunities. The RFG team will hold sessions to share stories, benefits and impact scenarios, discussions of current global and local events and trends, brainstorming, brainsteering, and mind mapping ses-sions around industry, market, and customer changes, including new knowledge for new opportunities. The team will also define decision parameters for quantifying, qualifying, and implementing suggestions.

Recognition, reward, and celebration of member contributions reinforce the intrapreneuring practice throughout the organization. The steps to set up an ongoing practice of reflection include:

1. Create the RFG team for routine reflecting, discussion, and seeking ideas for improvements and opportunities. Domains of reflection include operations outcomes, new opportunities, customer activity, and journaling insights.
2. Define a team charter that describes sessions, decision parameters, discussion and communication protocols, idea proposal guidelines, available resource budgeting, and a recognition and reward plan. Topics include:
   a. **Purpose and Objective:** includes the reason and desired result of the team effort.
   b. **Discussion Forums:** describes how, when, why, and where discussions will be held.
   c. **Team Members:** describes the protocol for who is involved in the team, including leadership responsibilities.
   d. **Parameters of Impact:** includes parameters that define the review guidelines for evaluating a suggested option or opportunity.
   e. **Protocols for Proposals:** provides a list of requirements to be included in an idea proposal, including preliminary qualifying/ quantifying research needed for consideration and estimation of costs of implementing a proposed idea.
   f. **Opportunity Leaders:** describes accountability and responsibility parameters for idea proposer and potential implementor.
   g. **Decision making:** provides a definition of decision-making parameters and timeframe.
   h. **Resource Allocation:** provides a definition of resources available for initial research and qualification/quantification of an idea; how and when resources can be acquired and allocated to implement an approved idea.
   i. **Recognition and Rewards:** describes how and why ideas will be accepted, recognized, and rewarded, celebrating new value.
   j. **Benefits/Impact Summary:** provides a benefits/impact summary to track the new value created, including cost or time savings,

new market, new customers, new revenue, new narrative, process improvement, employee or customer retention, and stakeholder motivation.

3. Schedule sessions to explore several domains that warrant reflection for intrapreneuring:

   a. Current narratives and mindset reviews of organization or individuals, including mindset components as they apply to current work and alignment to vision and mission goals

   b. Current work/projects' analyses of outcomes, workflow, benefits/ impact, and obstacles; current work that leads to ideas or opportunities to improve work and outcomes; or address new needs that are uncovered

   c. Unexpected successes or failures that suggest new opportunities

   d. Integration of operations workflows that suggest more efficiency and/or effectiveness, eliminating gaps and overlaps

   e. Continuous research of current trends, events, partner relationships, and new knowledges to identify new opportunities aligned with organization vision and mission; trends that suggest any change in direction, perspectives, and behaviors on a local or global scale; various catalysts that introduce a trend, such as Internet access to information, environmental factors, fashion updates, transportation modes, and communication vehicles

   f. Customer opportunity research that analyzes and evaluates their attributes, consumption chains, and contextual links; customers' mindsets and needs that suggest opportunities for new products and services within current scenarios, as well as creating new customers

   g. Recognizing and using invisible capital of members that solve problems or create new opportunities

   h. Review of individuals' journaling that suggests unexpected value created or opportunities for additional value

4. Hold brainstorming, brainsteering, and mind mapping sessions to uncover and refine ideas.

5. Hold sessions for quantifying and qualifying ideas using relevant data, information, and decision parameters that are guided by goals and values.

6. Hold recognition, reward, and celebration sessions to reinforce value creating work.
7. Provide an *Idea Box* with idea proposal requirements to collect any/all ideas that might add value. Monitor and discuss all submissions.

Mindset of Regular Reflection

Regular reflecting in all the aforementioned areas continuously reinforces the need to create new value. It creates a mindset that values this search and evaluation. It also recognizes the autonomy of members in taking control of their individual growth and survival and growth of their organization.

Suggested Research Sources

Ideas for improvement and new opportunities can be defined through reflection. However, in order to take advantage of these ideas and opportunities, they need to be researched to quantify and qualify them for feasibility and implementation. Research resources are many and are probably never defined by any one list. However, here is a proposed list to start your exploration of available data and information.

- U.S. government census
- Congressional Journal record of proceedings, votes, discussion points, and presentations
- Office of Management and Budget (OMB) for fiscal and monetary information
- Bureau of Labor Statistics (BLS)
- Other government databases
- Economic studies on specific topics noting trends and resulting changes
- Databases on any topic, collected and stored by institutes, associations, special task forces, and others
- Journals: academic and other of relevant research
- Articles: *NYT, WSJ, Bloomberg Businessweek, Forbes, The Economist, Smithsonian*, and others

- Conference proceedings with presentations, Q&A, speaker bios and background
- Association publications: professional, personal, and special interest

> **Do you evaluate the benefit of your reflections?**

- Consulting studies: basic academic research, practitioner research, and targeted client research
- Any other sources that are relevant to your idea, organization, or expertise

Paths of Reflection

As part of an autonomous environment, reflection is an imperative. It is integral to the fiber of knowledge work and skills. These reflective activities can be summarized as follows:

- Your narrative and mindset
- Project outcomes, benefits, and impact
- Integration of operations workflow
- Awareness of external new opportunities
- Customer activity and challenges
- Workers strengths and experiences as resources to introduce new value
- Journaling insights

Let's explore each domain to consider its value and understand how to benefit from each of them.

Your Narrative and Mindset

The first and, perhaps, the most important reflection is on your narrative. Your narrative is your story. It tells the story of who you are, your goals, what you value and believe, and how you are inclined to work with others. It can be intentional or unconscious. It also may be derailing you or helping you in your work with others. This reflection is the first opportunity to find needs for improvement or new value. You have your own narrative of self and the narrative that others hold of you. What do people think of you and your mindset? Does it align with your own perspective?

Your narrative is told through the artifacts of your beliefs, behaviors, and decisions. What artifacts today represent you and your narrative? Watch for others' reactions to you, your behaviors, and decisions. These reactions will mirror their narrative of you.

> *Pope John XXIII grew up in a poor family, the oldest of 13 children. His greatest joy was not school work but going to church. He entered the seminary at 12 years of age and diligently pursued a spiritual life of prayer, journaling his apprenticeship in spirituality. His practices of prayer, abstinence, avoidance of immodest expressions and readings, avoidance of bad companions, and special love for his peers were the artifacts that described his being. He was building a narrative of a saintly person but was also very curious about the world and the needs of the Catholic flock.*
>
> *Pope John XXIII was elected to the papacy at age 77. He had led a relatively quiet life with varying responsibilities. Pope Pius XII preceded Pope John XXIII with a very strong-handed control of church traditions, generating a significant influence that prevailed over Catholic church doctrines and practices. All expected John to follow in Pope Pius' pattern of leadership and to have a very uneventful tenure. John's narrative was predefined by others in this manner.*
>
> *John surprised church officials and the Catholic world with a significant impact as he led the church from 1958 to his death in 1963. He used his influence to challenge many unquestioned assumptions and initiated several changes to create a new presence for the Catholic church in the world. He maintained the foundational traditions of the church but integrated accommodations to modern times into that foundation. A new narrative was being shared with the Catholic world, one that was humanistic, unrelenting, and with no cynicism in his thoughts or actions. His peace within himself allowed him to inspire others. His flock felt this growth in his narrative as he changed it himself as a significant leader.*

Since stakeholders are all important to getting to your goals, it is essential to build their narrative of you. This means that you demonstrate artifacts, behaviors, and decisions that will tell your desired story of yourself.

Consider the (Grant 2021) communication/discussion personas of preacher, prosecutor, politician, or scientist approaches. Each persona will create a narrative around you and your intended values and beliefs. Are you usually a preacher, prosecutor, politician, or scientist when having a discussion with a colleague or stakeholder? Are you seeking to learn or tell? This differentiation makes a world of difference in what narrative you convey to others. Refer to Chapter 4 "Behavioral Concepts and Examples" for more detail on these discussion styles.

> **How often do you preach, prosecute, politicize, or inquire?**

Aligning Narrative Through Mindset

If you consider and then conclude that your narrative needs alteration, this alteration can be designed through your mindset. Your goals or your values or your beliefs or your mode of work might need a change in order to change your narrative.

When organization's and stakeholders' mindsets align with your own, work is streamlined to a common platform and the narrative is good. Trust, respect, and relationship are the result of this mindset alignment. Reflection on this alignment can happen routinely.

Lincoln had to analyze the mindset of his soldiers and generals who were weary of the war. He met them where they were on the battlefields to support them and use his engaging conversations to understand their thinking and keep them going. He reminded them of the common goal for which they were all sacrificing.

Your narrative is your entry ticket to effective and efficient knowledge work with stakeholders. You will not do anything more important than to manage this narrative. When your narrative needs to be modified, explore the origins of your narrative. What mindset components are no longer accurate or relevant? What would trigger a change to that component?

Compose a brief statement on the beliefs, behavioral tendencies, satisfiers, and motivators that will guide your decisions. Do they match those of your organization and stakeholders? Do these match your current project needs? Your narrative will be positive if they match. It will not be so good if it needs a change. Check others' reactions to evaluate that match.

Once John was chastised by church officials as being too adventurous because he was thought to have read a writing on modernism. This experience led him to a doctrine of moderation as opposed to modernism but he was still prone to integrate needed changes into the traditions of the church. John, when elected Pope, felt it necessary to integrate new needs, as society evolved, into traditional church doctrine. This defined his leadership approach, which was comforting to his worldwide flock and to church officials.

During John's evolving career and assignments, he was often silent when controversy presented itself on the debate of tradition versus modernism. His intent was to not demonstrate deviation from church orthodoxy. John didn't want the appearance of being at odds with Pope Pius XII's strict adherence to traditional church doctrine. He built his narrative as one of caring and kindness. When opportunity arose as pope, he used his chance to lead as he believed best for his flock with a mix of tradition and modernism.

Pope John's goals were in valuing humanity, regardless of religious sect or beliefs. He instituted the concept of Christians versus Catholics and also engaged people of all religions in his outreach.

Operational Outcomes

What outcomes of work or projects meet expected results or do not meet those expectations? Where is there an opportunity for improvement in those workflows?

Step 6, Implementing a Solution, of the learning system (refer to Chapter 7 "Ensuring Inquiry with a Learning System") provides a reflection point to identify the pros and cons of new work and its outcomes.

Did each step deliver the expected result? Reflecting and analyzing each situation can lead to insights for improvements or opportunities for something new to be created. Intrapreneuring and entepreneuring are possible given these insights. Formally, current work and projects can be analyzed in a Benefits/Impact summary that identifies outcomes. This Benefits/Impact Summary is presented in Figure 8.1.

Benefit/Impact	Sample Organization Details
Time Savings: (hours of work eliminated x $/hour)	Combined workflows
Cost Savings: (fees for materials and services eliminated)	Replaced text editing with a new text application
Revenue Generated: (new product or service delivery)	Added new automated customer service related to data entry
New Business Concepts: ($ from new products, new services, new customers minus costs)	Added new ancillary product to accompany main product, increasing distribution to a new market
New Business Pipeline: (potential $ from new customers)	Added new product use for a new customer base
Supporting Endeavors: (potential $ from supporting initiatives minus costs)	Added email service to phone services
Infrastructure Development: ($ generated from streamlining or enhancing delivery minus costs)	Created a new quality team to replace quality work within each operational workflow

Figure 8.1 Tracking outcomes—benefits and impact summary

Considering these benefits and their impact may provide ideas on other opportunities, which can be analyzed through step 2 of the learning system. In step 2, Entrepreneurial Options, an idea or opportunity is translated into a product or service that can be quantified and qualified in steps 3 and 4 of the learning system, respectively.

Step 2 of the learning system uncovers current and future options and opportunities. Some of these avenues are described in the following options.

Reflecting on Decision Rationale

When reflecting on current work and projects, it is helpful to reflect on your own and other's behaviors or decisions. What led to these behaviors and decisions? What mindset characteristic drove those behaviors and decisions?

What do you not know that you don't know? Do you know or do you think you know? Do you ever rethink what you think to be true (Grant 2021)? The consequences of not checking your thinking can be disastrous to an outcome. As change is continuous and consistent in our 21st century environment, reflection on that environment, your current mindset, actions, and decisions is essential. This includes a comprehensive review of actual and expected outcomes to find gaps to address. Grant gives an example of firefighters who followed routine operations when the nature of the fire was completely different than the usual scenario. Several firefighters lost their lives because they did not consider the current circumstances in order to behave differently to gain control of the fire.

Also, thinking in System One or System Two (Kahneman 2011) can help build a state of continuous reflection. System One is fast thinking, intuitive, and for emergency decisions. System Two is more delayed and deeper thinking, taking time to consider circumstances, options, outcomes, and new information. How do you determine the need for System One or System Two? What triggers each for you? Defining decision parameters can help define the best response situationally. Routine reflection, System One or System Two, quick or delayed, can all bring new insights to drive your actions and decisions. When you reflect on a new scenario, a change in goal or approach to work and decisions may be suggested.

Reflecting on Stakeholders' Goals and Values

Stakeholder's goals and values are an integral part of your work with them. Considering them in real time helps not only with current work alignment but also with insights into your own goals and values. How do you perceive stakeholder's behaviors and decisions? Do these remind you of yourself or of others? Consider how others see you in the context of how you see others. Are there aspects of your behaviors and decisions that you would like to change? Could neural mirrors, decision influencers, or choice architectures be helpful in these situations?

Pope John's story, as told over the decades of his leadership in the Catholic church, accommodated tradition and modernity at the same time. His goal was to promote the humanity present in all members of the church community.

John's multiple encyclicals demonstrated the artifacts of his narrative and purpose in life. His statements were aimed at "all men of good will." He addressed all areas of social reform, as well as an end to the nuclear arms race among other worldwide needs. His topics depicted his mindset explicitly, one of inclusion and compromise.

He further demonstrated his narrative with his engagement of all people in the same way no matter their status or background. He was a friend to all in equal measure.

Reflecting on the Benefit/Impact Summary

Routinely, a record of all work and impact should be kept as benefits to an individual and an organization. Discussion of these impacts can lead to other opportunities.

> **Do you consider the impact you have had to yourself and/or your organization?**

Table 8.1 suggests the sample Benefit/Impact Summary of an intern working for a host organization. His impacts are described:

Table 8.1 Intern benefits/impact summary

Benefit/Impact	Company Details
Time Savings	By working on a search for potential clients, I was able to help the firm define and set up three new channels to reach out to new ventures seeking funding. This saved the company time to work on other big projects and not worry about allocating a lot of time to work on applications. Through my plan I was integral in establishing a new and repeatable outreach process for a future business analyst.
Cost Savings	My internship was unpaid and I also helped the firm to save money on hiring a new analyst and training costs since I picked up everything fast and worked independently.

(Continued)

Table 8.1 (Continued)

Benefit/Impact	Company Details
Revenue Generated	With my help of finding potential clients and performing a cold call with them, the company gained over 200 new applications and closed 3 deals. Those 3 deals have great potential. Based on the financial documentations, they will bring a lot of profit to the investors.
New Business Concepts	Although my project didn't generate new business concepts, I helped the firm to establish a new approach of outreach for potential clients.
New Business Pipeline	Over the last 4 months, Company X generated over 200 new funding applications, all due to my approach of channel selection. In the future, this will help the company to stay consistent with the number of applications coming in and will save time for the new business analysts performing outreach to potential clients.
Supporting Endeavors	I hope that Company X will utilize my method of outreach and channel selection to help them generate more and more funding applications in the future.
Add others who are relevant to one's project	XXXXXX

Integration of Operations

Operational departments design their own workflows to meet their outcomes. Their goal is to be efficient and effective in meeting the outcomes needed by themselves and, potentially, by the other operational departments. There is, however, the possibility that when examined as an overarching workflow of the organization, there could be overlaps, gaps, or obstacles uncovered. These discoveries present the opportunity to integrate workflows for better efficiencies. These insights allow the organizational departments to share or repurpose resources toward better outcomes for the organization as a whole. Do you or your organization have overlaps, gaps, or obstacles that might be improved? Queries might include:

a. Where are the connections between operational entities, their stakeholders, contributors, and functional roles?

b. Where could these entities help each other with efficiency or effectiveness?

c. How do these entities impact each other with planned inputs and outcomes?

> **Do you consult your network of colleagues to find improvements to the workflow?**

This process builds productive relationships across functional areas for best overarching performance.

Global, Industry, Market Trends, Events, and Activities

What is going on in your world that could impact you or your organization? Reflecting on these occurrences can be systematized to include global, industry, and market events, trends, and activities. Do they suggest an opportunity to intrapreneur or entrepreneur?

Seven Frames of Opportunity

Seven contexts potentially provide opportunities to improve operations or create new value (Drucker 1985). Focusing reflection on internal and external conditions and events can point to new value to be created. An unexpected failure of a project gives insights into what would make the project more successful. A world change in supply chain practices could eliminate bottlenecks that harm economic growth. A failed product launch and its exploration can lead to an entirely new business model that will be very successful. Reflections can identify small and large problems, as well as small and large opportunities to modify behaviors and decisions. They also help you check for alignment to your vision, mission, and project goals.

Finally, reflecting on global events and conditions can uncover an unforeseen problem of the future for a current project. This insight is invaluable. Reflective brainstorming, brainsteering, and mind mapping in these contexts will help identify events and trends in the following domains:

a. **Unexpected success or failure:** catalyst to root-cause analysis to identify new or existing need

b. **Incongruities:** discrepancy between what is and what ought to be or between what is and what people assume to be

c. **Process Need:** improve an existing process, replace a weak link, or redesign for greater efficiency

d. **Industry and Market Structures:** national to global presence, new technology impact, and customer new orientations

e. **Demographics:** social, philosophical, political, and intellectual environment changes

f. **Changes in Perception:** fad, trend, or new awareness of a need

g. **New Knowledge:** combination of knowledges coming together, when a new idea finally takes hold

Queries might include:

a. Where do organizational products and services add value to a trend, event, or customer?

b. What trend or event impacts your customers, present or future?

c. What trend, event, or customer presents a new opportunity to explore?

d. Are any market structures evolving in ways that can present a new opportunity to explore?

e. Are customers', present and/or future, mindsets presenting opportunities or new needs?

f. What changes in demographics, perceptions, or new knowledge are currently happening?

The Chinese recognized that they needed to modernize their automobile industry with updated German performance standards. This initiative

| Where might you contribute to a world trend or event? |

was a cultural transition before it was a business project. But the Chinese saw value in the Western mode of industrial work and wanted to take advantage of the current practices of the Germans. They made allowances for a new Western mindset to prevail, even though it was difficult to accommodate new practices and mindsets. The opportunity for growth was too significant to not engage.

Customer Activity

Exploring who your customers are and what practices are important to them can introduce new ways to serve them. What customer activities might present an opportunity for new value within that customer domain? Brainstorming and/or brainsteering on customers and their activities includes three considerations to get to know your customers and their needs more clearly. They include contextual links, attributes, and consumption chain needs (MacMillan and McGrath 2000). Exploratory questions might include:

a. What is the context within which your customers live, survive, and thrive?
b. What are the specific attributes of different customer groups?
c. What are the consumption chains of your customers?

Customer Context

What does your customer's world look like? Who are their customers? What are the industry descriptors that impact them or their customers? Are opportunities growing for them? Is there an obstacle in their domains that may cause them difficulties? How are they faring with global changes and challenges? Answering these questions may uncover opportunities that had previously not been considered.

Customer Attributes

Can you describe your customer's attributes for each of them? How do these attributes create obstacles or advantages for them? How might you enhance these attributes for them? How would these enhancements change your relationship with them as customers? Answers often equal potential new opportunities.

Customer Consumption Chain

Observing how, where, and when your customers conduct themselves or their businesses can give you insights into opportunities to streamline

> **Do you collaborate with customers for building trust, relationship, and new value?**

or improve their flow of business. Do you see any opportunities as you study their overarching workflows? Are there difficulties or costs that you could help remove? Do your customers need help in maximizing opportunities that might come up in their workflows or relationships? Answers often equal potential new opportunities.

Individual Profiles

Who works alongside you or within your organization? As all autonomous knowledge workers have their profiles ready for reference, it is easy to seek and engage the strengths, interests, and invisible capital of members to broaden goals, solve problems, or create new opportunities.

Organizational members and partners' profiles can introduce some untapped resources for the organization. Using these resources is motivational and value creating for the individual members and for the organization. Refer to Chapter 5 "Your Goals and Values" for detailed descriptions of profiles.

> **Do you seek to maximize your own and others' talents and expertise?**

Brainstorm, brainsteer, and mind map individuals' strengths, interests, and expertise as invisible capital (Raab 2010) to broaden your goals or those of your project or organization. This invisible capital is useful as an insightful resource and for making connections for solving problems. Questions include:

a. Who do you know who is familiar with a situation or environment connected to your issue or opportunity? Who within your organization might have a strength in this area?

b. What do you know yourself that is related to this issue or opportunity? What do you need to know? Who else might be helpful with these knowledges?

c. What might you be involved in that is related to this issue or opportunity? What are others involved in that would be relevant to your issue or opportunity?

Journaling

Daily and brief individual journaling records unexpected occurrences and opportunities to recognize new value created and how to use it for additional value. What have workers observed and recorded in their journals that provides insight into an improvement or a new idea?

The practice of journaling is helpful to individuals, as well as to projects and organizations. It systematizes individual reflection and creates a record of reactions and impressions in real time. When, why, and where do workers journal? How is it used to share insights and ideas? What have workers observed and recorded in their journals that might provide insight into current or future work, an improvement, or a new idea? Journaling can actually focus on all of the domains mentioned here to ensure comprehensive thinking and rethinking of current activities.

Having a structured approach to journaling can initiate thoughts that might otherwise be lost. Journaling provides continuous atten-

> **Is journaling a part of your routine life?**

tion to sensitivities, rewards, causes, current and upcoming problems, or, perhaps, new needs to be fulfilled. When journaling includes mindset considerations, many new needs and opportunities become apparent, recognizing that growth often happens from the mindset perspective. Figure 8.2 gives a foundational description of a journaling activity.

Date	Thinking	Rethinking
9/28/22	Today's thoughts: What happened?	Why it happened?
	Today's wins: What went well?	Why it happened and what would make it even better?
	Today's challenges: What went badly?	Why it happened and what could have been better?
	Yesterday's thoughts: What got better today?	Why did it seem better today?

Figure 8.2 Journaling

Celebrations

Celebration comes in many forms. It includes all the references in this chapter for recognition and rewards. But what is recognition and what is a reward?

Recognition is any instance of acknowledgment of some progress made. Noting someone's work as it aligns to a communication protocol or decision-making challenge is considered recognition. Acknowledgment can be empowering, especially as it reinforces a job well done in the presence of others. This recognition can come from anyone who has knowledge of another's contribution.

Reward is a more formal recognition of a positive impact or some growth achieved. It includes a certificate, a monetary reward, a new opportunity, or perhaps a letter of commendation. It is coveted by organizational members and reinforces the mental model of the community.

Individuals and organizations reinforce and celebrate positive work with recognition and rewards, and so this work continues. It celebrates the autonomous mindset that is essential to the 21st century knowledge economy.

Worksheet Reference

Worksheets to facilitate using the concepts in this chapter are found in "Developing the Intentional Mindset, Module 6: Reflecting and Celebrating." The worksheets include:

Journaling
Reflections for Growth (RFG) Team Charter
Growth Parameters, Investment, and Returns Parameters
Story/Project Session Planning
Narrative Check-In
Benefits/Impact, New Opportunity Analysis

Call to Action

Consider your world as you can envision it to create your most attractive life. List the factors that could influence this condition.

1. Think about how you can shape these influences to create that most attractive life.
2. Check that your mindset is aligned with this life.

3. Celebrate all activity that has created something of value.

4. Reflect on your reflections and what they yield.

5. In what reflective areas do you focus?

6. Do you reflect routinely?

7. What do you celebrate?

8. Do you need to systematize your reflections with a journaling approach to support your growth into an attractive life?

Chapter Summary

This chapter describes the practice of comprehensive reflection and several potential paths for consideration. The next chapter describes the organizational environment needed to facilitate the autonomous work required in the 21st century knowledge economy.

Building an Environment to Support Autonomous Work

CHAPTER 9

Building an Autonomous Environment

Do you feel a comfort level when working? Is it always clear what you should work on? How you should work? How much decision making is entrusted to you? The actual vision, mission, goals, and values of your organization? What you are striving for yourself? How should you pursue that direction? Is it possible to pursue that direction within your organization?

> **Autonomy and 21st century knowledge work can't survive without an autonomous environment.**

Managers and leaders have the responsibility to ensure that expectations of autonomous work are understood, organizational direction and goals are clear, and an autonomous mode of work is integrated into the environment. Besides these, a critical component of this environment is the digital nervous system, which provides all data and information needed for decision making. Autonomous knowledge work needs an environment that supports its workers. They will not be able to do their most productive work for the organization and achieve its goals without this supportive environment.

An autonomous environment is intentionally designed and implemented to clarify organizational expectations and supporting functions that impact an individuals' work. It exists for creating a common platform that builds awareness and management of mindset in order to maximize individual productivity and organizational performance.

The key ideas discussed in this chapter include:

- An environment for success
- Vision, mission, and goals
- The framework of autonomy

- Knowledge work templates
- Building an autonomous narrative for your organization
- Organizational structures and narrative

An Environment for Success

Recognizing your own goals and values provides great context and direction for your thinking. Also, all work should include a goal and a sense of some compatible value. Otherwise, you may find yourself just working in a vacuum with no real guidance. How do you know that you are headed toward success? How do others know what you are striving for and how they can help you? What do you and others need to be thinking in order to achieve a goal? This is the common mindset of a goal and values that sparks effective and collaborative work. In an organization, your mindset is accompanied by the organization's mindset. These common mindsets enable best productivity toward joint goals.

The environment that enables this work is important. It is intentional and focused on a sacred and valued goal and direction. This is not an environment that can be left to chance. It is intentionally designed, created, and maintained. The 21st century knowledge work must be learning and knowledge-oriented, inclusive of all perspectives, and structured in a way that facilitates the independent and dependent work of autonomy.

Success happens when the right or lucky environment is in place (Frank 2016). This environment includes certain conditions that need to be present. Some people are born into this environment but others need to develop it for themselves. It is in the context of your goals and values that you can create this environment for yourself. Learning and awareness of your mindset components ensures that work and decisions will lead to the outcomes you desire. You and/or organizational leaders have to create the environment to enable this learning, both for individuals and for organizations.

Aligning Leadership and an Autonomous Environment

To set the stage for an autonomous environment to exist, leaders have to value and believe in the ability of organizational members to be autonomous, self-sufficient, and learning and growth-oriented. Recognizing the need to build and support trusting and productive relationships with internal and external stakeholders is a first priority for ensuring satisfaction and motivation. Which management theories (Sachs 2022; Ouchi 1981) make the best sense to facilitate your stakeholders' efforts? Theory X for continuous direction? Theory Y for self-direction toward stated goals? Theory Z for individual motivation, development, and growth? A leader may use a combination of these theories but should be conscious of when, where, and how to use each for building trust and relationship. What are the artifacts in the organization that will demonstrate these theories, as needed?

Vision, Mission, and Goals

Sharing the relevance of vision, mission, and goals for work is essential in building an autonomous environment. Initiatives or projects have mission goals that incrementally support vision goals of the organization. How are these goals related to your vision for yourself? This query and its answer gives perspective to your overall effort. Organizational perspective brings workers to the same common platform for working tougher.

Goals and values set the stage and direction to develop the beliefs and mode of work needed to achieve progress in any pursuit. Inquiry into the organizational mindset/narrative gives the autonomous worker context and a framework for planning work to be effective. An organization sets up this goal and value structure to provide expectations and a common platform to align all workers to others in the organization. When all workers are aware of this context, work is streamlined toward a common consensus of what, why, when, and how work should proceed and decisions to be made. Individual development planning is correlated to the plans of the organization, as well.

The Framework of Autonomy

An organizational model of autonomy is described by the components of a learning environment (Kleiner et al. 1994). This environment includes five organizational structures:

- **Personal mastery:** ensuring that all members have a personal profile and development plan for personal and professional growth, community contributions, and individual expertise

- **Mental models:** engaging all members in current organizational mindset components
- **Shared vision:** sharing with members the organization's vision and mission
- **Team learning:** building a common platform for team efforts with learning expectations and work protocols
- **Systems thinking:** identifying opportunities for organizational and external systems to integrate with each other for new value creation

These frameworks, as described in Table 9.1, are made tangible with the following functions provided by an organizational leader. Following are the details of the functions of an autonomous environment.

Table 9.1 The framework of autonomy

Autonomy Components	Autonomy Environment, Protocols, Decisions	Autonomous Functions
Personal Mastery	Personal, professional, community, and expert profiles; growth and learning planning	1. Profiling and maximizing individual strengths 2. Ensuring satisfiers and motivators 3. Instilling inquiry and learning perspectives: data and decisions 4. Sharing decision-making expectations
Mental Models	Values, beliefs, and mode of work, stakeholder integration, decision parameters	1. Implementing theories X, Y, Z 2. Getting to a result 3. Building mindset awareness: self and stakeholders 4. Collaborating using social experiences 5. Reinforcing persistence 6. Facilitating community mentality, aligning mindsets with archetype analysis, decision influencers, and choice architectures 7. Reinforcing and rewarding new ideas and value 8. Retaining customers and employees

Autonomy Components	Autonomy Environment, Protocols, Decisions	Autonomous Functions
Shared Vision	Organizational mindset for creating new value, goal sharing	1. Providing context of organizational vision, mission, mindset, and compelling narrative 2. Supporting growth-oriented, new value creations, percent of revenue from new value created 3. Implementing a Reflections for Growth Team (RFG) 4. Sharing, reflecting on, and celebrating experiences and scenarios
Team Learning	Data and information, decisions, digital nervous system, learning system structure, projects	1. Defining metrics and measures 2. Implementing collaborative brain functioning 3. Allocating budget and resources 4. Maximizing communication 5. Using project structures, teams, and charters 6. Using the learning system 7. Providing data and information (digital nervous system) for autonomous work 8. Providing decision responsibilities and parameters
Systems Thinking	Reflections, pivots, autonomous environment, recognition and rewards	1. Reviewing operational systems for integration 2. Reviewing and reflecting on cases/projects for pivots 3. Reflecting on and maximizing individual and organizational strengths 4. Tracking outcomes to uncover new opportunities and to guide recognition and rewards 5. Reviewing current global, regional, industry, and local events and trends to uncover new opportunities

Personal Mastery

The personal mastery component of an autonomous organization includes individual planning around mindset, growth, destiny, and legacy.

PM 1: Profiling and Maximizing Individual Strengths

Individual knowledge workers have a plan for what each would like to achieve and the path to get to those goals, long term and short term. Each member creates a profile that is posted within the organization resources for all to access. The profile includes the individual's goals, values, beliefs, strengths, interests, and mode of work. Activities, projects, and progress are added and updated on a regular basis for all to reference when looking for ideas or resources to help create new value.

Knowledge workers need to create their own plans for their growth, destiny, legacy, and work. This should foster innovative ideas for the organization to grow along with them.

PM 2: Ensuring Satisfiers and Motivators

Satisfiers and motivators are both important but serve different needs for knowledge workers. Herzberg and his colleagues defined hygiene satisfiers and motivators (Nickerson 2021). Hygiene factors can satisfy or dissatisfy workers causing short-term changes in job attitude and performance, as well as retention. They include factors of company policy, supervisor relationships, interpersonal relations, working conditions, and salary. Motivation factors, however, cause longer-term positive job performance. They include growth factors of achievement, opportunities, advancement, recognition, the work itself, and responsibility.

Satisfiers, specifically compensation and working conditions, are transparent between the knowledge worker and the organization. It is important that industry standard compensation schedules are referenced and used to set acceptable salaries and benefits. Working conditions should also remove obstacles to knowledge work autonomy. Motivators are more complex and need continuous attention to keep these factors current and adjustable depending on knowledge worker mindsets.

Satisfiers and motivators are created by the leader's attitude toward work and workers. Leaders must support and sustain knowledge work with awareness and implementation of satisfiers and, then, with motivators related to their members' growth and planning for the future. Consider that motivation is a value that depends on organizational and leader beliefs and behaviors.

Asplund and Brim (2023) discuss various elements for building strong employee engagement, such as measuring engagement with meaningful inquiry, having growth-oriented conversations, providing clear and ongoing communications, focusing on well-being, and having strengths-based conversations.

To the contrary, demotivators (Meyer 1978) include:

- Lack of constructive feedback
- Inconsistent behavior by those who directly affect success
- Lack of sensitivity to individual needs
- Denial of sufficient information
- Intrusion (interference) into predefined psychological and actual job space
- Psychological contracts, made during interview discussions, for mutual agreement between employer and employees that address mostly satisfiers and not motivators
- Employee orientation delays causing misinformation due to self-constructed orientation

If an employee only seeks satisfaction and not motivation, productivity will be limited and growth will not be a priority for that person.

PM 3: Instilling Inquiry and Learning: Data and Decisions

The growth of personal mastery is based on curiosity. Leaders must encourage this curiosity by demonstrating an inquiry approach to all considerations, discussions, and decisions. Data and information must be provided for research of inquiries for learning to occur. Decisions are understood to be data-driven.

Forums for decision-making and collaborative discussions are held as needed and anyone can informally convene a discussion. Decisions can be checked with a peer for validation or thinking as a common practice.

When a new employee has a question regarding a process, customer, or product, it is often answered with another question to guide inquiry and personal discovery.

PM 4: Sharing Decision-Making Expectations

In an autonomous 21st century environment, everyone makes decisions. Specific decision-making responsibility is defined with ranges of possible outcomes that are acceptable. This guidance helps knowledge workers with expectations of autonomous behaviors and context for decision making.

Often, decisions have many perspectives to consider especially in a team setting. One subject-matter expert who is closest to an issue usually has the responsibility of making the decision based on collaborative input. The leader defines who is responsible for a decision and the range of acceptability based on the organization's vision, mission, and goals.

Mental Models

Building mental models for organizational members enables them to think based on a common mindset of goals, values, beliefs, and mode of work.

MM1: Implementing Theories X, Y, and Z

Management theories help to design the work environment that will maximize worker autonomy and productivity (Sachs 2022; Ouchi 1981). MacGregor defined theory X and theory Y. Theory X states that individual workers need continuous direction on what to work on and how to work. It assumes that workers are not thinking people who can be self-directed and decision makers in their work. Theory Y states that workers need only the direction of goals and are quite capable of defining their work requirements and mode of work to achieve those goals.

William Ouchi added theory Z to these theories. Theory Z notes that employee satisfaction and motivation promote high productivity. Theory Z is based on leader commitment to long-term employment and focus on support for the complete well-being and growth of employees.

Leaders, consciously or unconsciously, selectively align with these theories to create modes of work for their workers. The theories may be used situationally based on the intent and goal of the work. Leaders' mindsets direct these choices and, therefore, the productivity and creativity of employees.

MM2: Getting to a Result

Recognizing the importance of getting to a result is an essential aspect of knowledge work. What is the result you are seeking with every effort? How do you know that you have reached that result? Leaders set this expectation in an autonomous environment. Is the result focused on learning or performance goals? What is the best mode of work to get to that result? And is the result or is the process of achieving that result more important?

Every effort should have a concept of the result expected. This assures that efforts and work are meaningful and not just filling time with peripheral work. And the knowledge worker feels accomplishment and confidence with a tangible result.

MM3: Building Mindset Awareness: Self and Stakeholders

Mindset holds great power. Recognizing this importance, awareness, and alignment within an organization is a major influencer toward success. Inquiry into your own and stakeholders' mindsets is essential in order to align them for commonality in decision making. A large percentage of decisions are based on mindset, so if mindsets don't align, decisions will not align with the common direction of organizational goals. If values and beliefs differ, decisions will be conflicted by these different perspectives. Also, if your mode of work doesn't match your own goals, values, or beliefs, then actions will conflict and cause failure and significant confusion.

MM4: Collaborating Using Social Experiences

Current research of Workforce Intelligence (Schawbel 2018) notes that social experiences enhance workers' productivity and performance toward goals and happiness. An autonomous organization provides opportunities for social experiences among knowledge workers routinely. If members of an organization are to work effectively, social experiences provide the opportunity to meet and understand stakeholders in order to work as they build trust and relationship. Coffee hours, cocktail events, and roundtable discussions led by volunteers are all social experiences.

Since autonomous work is as much about your stakeholders as about yourself, opportunities to delve into others' mindsets support the ability to design work and goals that will be aligned with all mindsets, which is the most expeditious manner of work.

When people socialize and get to know each other, mindsets are not an obstacle. They know how each other thinks, values, believes, and works to predict what will or will not be acceptable. They are not threatened by the unknown.

MM5: Reinforcing Persistence

Persistence can be supported by the readiness, relevance, reinforcement, and reflection (RRRR) staging of communication and a hierarchy of goals. (Refer to Maximizing Communication below.) These techniques provide continuous feedback to keep engagement high and results assured. Persistence is also supported through recognition and reward structures to reinforce autonomous work, decision making, and positive outcomes meeting the hierarchy of goals.

When road blocks are numerous and threaten continued commitment on a project, a leader's attention to pivots and persistence is often what will save a project. Recognizing and rewarding all attempts to derail roadblocks, and not penalizing failed attempts, should be routine.

A hierarchy of goals also supports persistent efforts since achievement is incremental and easier to attain.

MM6: Facilitating Community Mentality, Aligning Mindsets With Archetype Analysis, Decision Influencers, and Choice Architectures

Community mentalities are formed by the mindsets of members. This includes all of the behaviors and decisions that align with them. A community mindset might be a belief that work with nonmembers is unacceptable due to their lack of expertise. Another community mindset might be a belief in hoarding information to enhance the exclusivity of the expertise of the members. A third mindset might value mentoring of colleagues who are not members of the community for sharing expertise. A fourth mindset might so highly value the performance standards of a specific discipline, such as engineering or scientific research, that the members of that community might not be flexible enough to pivot for adjustment to another mode of work. Finally, a particular religious group might have no tolerance for working with others from another religious orientation.

Leaders have the responsibility to ensure that these differing mindsets can work together without conflicts that cause obstacles to achieving the goals of the organization. Archetype workflow analysis can diagnose the cause of an obstacle. Decision influencers and choice architectures can help to align the mindsets to eliminate the obstacle.

Community mindsets may be helpful to knowledge work and a specific project or they might be detrimental to progress. Environmental factors of recognition, reward, or accountability within an organization can support or diffuse these mindsets as needed to align with the organization's mindset.

MM7: Reinforcing and Rewarding New Ideas and Value

Providing a framework, protocols, and requirements for evaluating new ideas encourages organizational members to be creative in intrapreneuring. A framework includes a team to hold brainstorming, brainsteering, and mind mapping sessions focused on current events and trends, as well as customer conditions and needs. Protocols and requirements include the structures around how, when, and why these sessions are held and decisions are made. They include the range of considerations, evaluation of potential value to be created, and costs associated with implementing an idea.

MM8: Retaining Customers and Employees

All organizational members are focused on stakeholders' mindsets in order to meet or modify expectations to achieve common goals. Customers and employees are considered stakeholders and collaborators. All members are aware of how to match stakeholder expectations or how to help modify the expectations for a common platform to guide work toward the common goal. Retaining stakeholders is key to the stability and sustainability of self and the organization.

Shared Vision

Sharing vision with organizational members provides the context for a common direction of vision and mission to guide work and new value creation.

SV1: Providing Context of Organizational Vision, Mission, Mindset, and Compelling Narrative

Leaders share the organization's vision, mission, values, beliefs, goals, and mode of work. Essentially, they provide a narrative of the organization to guide members' thinking and work.

When knowledge workers are working autonomously, they use the narrative context of the organizational vision, mission, and mindset to guide their thinking and decision making. When conflicts arise within teams, the shared vision is a great resource for bringing the work back to a common platform.

SV2: Supporting Growth-Oriented, New Value Creations, Percent of Revenue From New Value Created

Setting the expectation that all work should be focused on creating growth, guides knowledge workers to achieve a growth result with each task. Daily work is important in this context. It should be approached with the metric and measure of the goal in mind that will contribute to the hierarchy of goals that supports the organization's higher level goals. Revenue realized is also reported.

SV3: Implementing a Reflections for Growth Team

The knowledge-oriented organization can spark growth thinking with a formalized team that sets up and monitors reflective growth thinking for all organizational members. The Reflections for Growth (RFG) team holds regular discussion sessions for considering current events and trends, customer needs and trends, and reviews of current work and projects that may provide opportunities to improve outcomes. There is no limit to what can be discussed and topics, trends, or events can be suggested by any organizational member.

The RFG team also provides a process for proposing ideas and for evaluating them against a range of decision parameters, use of resources, and amount of value to be created. The team also maintains records of discussions, ideas proposed, and results. There is also a recognition and rewards structure for celebrating intrapreneurial thinking and work, including full disclosure of the actual value created.

SV4: Sharing, Reflecting on, and Celebrating Experiences and Scenarios

Sharing work-related stories and experiences often uncovers opportunities that might not be thought about by any one individual. Depending on individual profiles and interests, discussion can be very diverse, introducing new ideas for consideration. Individuals are likely to have skills or expertise in these diverse domains, which the organization should maximize. When people share their insights with each other, there is a compilation of perspectives that can lead to ideas and opportunities that would otherwise not be considered.

Team Learning

Setting expectations for team learning empowers members to be effective collaborators, decision makers, and knowledge workers who seek data and information to quantify and qualify their decisions. All initiatives are structured as a project, facilitated with defined collaboration protocols and joint decision making.

TL1: Defining Measures and Metrics

Team and project work is governed by the metric of what is to be achieved and what needs to be measured to get to that metric. What will determine team work as a success or a failure? What metric will make that case? And how will that metric be measured on a routine basis? There are industry and competitor metrics that can be considered to align for industry recognition, as well.

Usually, the purpose and objective of the project define this metric, which can be learning or performance-based. The measures to track that metric are defined by the knowledge workers as they conduct their daily work.

TL2: Implementing Collaborative Brain Function

Recent studies show higher brain performance by people who work together in a social setting (Zynga 2014). It doesn't matter what the social activity might be, the participants in these groups outperform the individuals who work alone. Brain functions are enhanced by social modes of work in a collaborative environment that readily engages knowledge workers. Workers who socialize build trust and relationship that makes working together more compatible and makes it easier to reach common goals. Productivity is the result of this collaborative environment.

TL3: Allocating Budgets and Resources

Growth and value creation are incentivized with adequate resources to support these efforts. Time and money should be allocated for reflection and review of various domains, internal and external to the organization. An innovation budget will include funds for thinking time, research time, and resources for new project implementation. These amounts are set based on the feasibility of a new creation and speculated return on investment, which are evaluated by the RFG team and the proposer of an idea.

TL4: Maximizing Communication

Communication standards and protocols that are strictly used and reinforced can ensure that all are working from the same set of beliefs and mindset. Readiness, relevance, reinforcement, and reflection (RRRR) stages of communication set the expectation for communication practices to ensure awareness and engagement. These stages categorize communication into four sequential areas that answer all questions and streamline collaborative work. The sequence includes:

- **Readiness:** Who needs to be prepared to work on an initiative? What do they need to know to join the team?
- **Relevance:** What information, goals, and protocols of work will be helpful in engaging in their distinct and defined roles?
- **Reinforcement:** Who and what will assure that team members are satisfied and motivated to continue with their most conscientious efforts?
- **Reflection:** What work goals should be met and when? What are metrics and measures that will be tracked? What obstacles need to be removed to improve work to meet desired metrics? What changes need to be made? Economically? Mindset?

The benefits of RRRR staging include alignment of workers, availability of needed resources, time savings, and retention of workers through continuous communication for clarity, engagement, and commitment.

When a project is initiated, team members are better engaged when the communication connects the purpose, goal, potential impact, and desired result of the project prior to the start of work.

The functional purpose of communications is to recognize, share, and value expectations. Well-intended people often find themselves in conflict with their stakeholders because they have different expectations on goals or outcomes desired. Often, this conflict is the result of people having different beliefs or modes of work that lead to diverse decisions.

Simplicity (Jensen 2000) presents a plan for building the RRRR stages of communicating. It includes communicating in the context of your stakeholders and their needs for information. Communication is not two-way but four-way. You speak from your own mindset/perspective, another listens from his unique mindset/perspective, you hear and respond from the context of your mindset, and, finally, the listener hears the response from his mindset/perspective. The conversation is now on two different tracks, often even talking on two totally different topics.

Check Chapter 2 "Defining Mindset Components" for a detailed description of Jensen's communications plan. According to Jensen, a sure way to avoid this diversion is to understand the mindset of your listener prior to making a point or talking at all. Asking yourself, "What will he hear when I say *XXX*?" will help you to modify the message to be meaningful in the way that you intend. Data/decision influencers or a choice architecture can help with the construct of your messaging that will be persuasive to the mindset of the listener.

To clarify, RRRR stages of communication present the framework for communicating and Jensen presents a plan for crafting the messages in each of these stages of communication.

Communication protocols for any organization can be constructed in support of the organizational values. How do those values translate into communication practices and protocols to guide all work activities?

Communication is the underlying factor in motivating people to be learners and responsible knowledge workers. They will subsequently always be ready to create new value when presented with the opportunity. Project structures and the learning system steps guide this work.

TL5: Using Project Structures, Teams, and Charters

Project thinking and structures provide a framework of sequencing work steps to keep movement persistent toward the goal. It is a way to approach all work with a common platform, setting expectations for the flow of work. The readiness, relevance, reinforcement, and reflection (RRRR) stages of communication are built into the framework and are helpful for progressing seamlessly from step to step with all stakeholders involved, as necessary, with clarity of purpose and implementation of work.

Projects are systematically implemented to ensure good decision making, using behavioral and traditional economic principles and platforms. Stakeholders' assumptions, beliefs, and biases are identified, analyzed, and satisfied with insightful communication. Projects are defined by a project charter that describes the project in detail, including team members and their roles and responsibilities. A sample project charter describes the RFG team in Chapter 8 "Reflections, New Value, and Celebrations.

TL6: Using the Learning System

Chapter 7 "Ensuring Inquiry With a Learning System" provides a full detailed description of how a learning system is used. All work and activities follow the six learning system steps so that all considerations and evaluations are done systematically. Work steps are guided by templates and expected outcomes as input to the next step. The steps include:

1. Building mindset awareness
2. Entrepreneuring/intrapreneuring for creating new value
3. Testing economic feasibility
4. Testing emotional/mindset feasibility
5. Implementing with a project structure
6. Reflecting on outcomes, options, and opportunities for creating new value

TL7: Providing Data and Information (Digital Nervous System) for Autonomous Work

A digital nervous system (Gates 1999) supports inquiry and research for all knowledge work activity. It starts with basic data collection on sales, operations, customer activity and behaviors, competitive forces, industry and market practices and operations, and general supply/consumption chain activity. Individual profiles are also available for data and information on strengths, interests, and experiences of organizational members, customers, and competitors. Current events, trends, industry, and census data and information are also available in the digital nervous system to provide the context for internal as well as external innovative decisions.

These data and information components can be pivoted to provide specific perspectives to answer additional queries as relevant to a project or goal. These resources are unending and are sparked by the creativity of the inquirer. Understanding obstacles to reaching a goal, such as mindsets, can lend insight into the inquiry that will guide data and information pivots for gaining clarity on a project's needs.

A digital nervous system, similar to the nervous system of a human body, makes data and information easily available for uncovering interdependencies and potential solutions to obstacles. Inquiry and learning are supported by this approach so that data-driven decisions are the norm. Data can be collected for easy access and reference while working and making decisions. It can then be filtered and pivoted to answer questions that provide deeper clarity around obstacles or dilemmas.

Data and information to diagnose mindsets and guide modifications are also available for aligning thinking when needed, as well. An inventory of stakeholders' mindsets as currently defined is also available for reference.

Data and information sources can include:

- Current events and trends
- News stories
- Academic journal articles
- Nonfiction books
- Op/Ed articles
- Industry journal articles
- Government-sponsored databases
- Talking to associates and friends about their goals and values
- Understanding your own and others' mindsets
- Understanding customer mindset, attributes, consumption chain, and contextual links
- Combination of any of these sources and their workflows
- Individual and stakeholder profiles, including narratives and invisible capital
- Operational data
- Sales and customer purchasing data
- Customer data on trends and needs
- Census data on potential customers
- Geographic data on locations and related markets and customers

TL8: Providing Decision Responsibilities and Parameters

Decisions are critical to autonomous knowledge work. In the context of project or team work, decision responsibilities should be defined, as well as some parameters for making those decisions. Decision responsibilities are defined according to levels of overall knowledge in the decision area. For example, work decisions within a cross-functional team are usually made by the subject-matter expert closest to the decision area.

Parameters define the range of acceptable use of resources, expected return on investment, and when exceptions can be considered. Parameters are set by organizational leaders and implemented by autonomous knowledge workers.

Systems Thinking

Thinking in a systems mode enables the knowledge worker to see the connections between work resources, workflow, and stakeholders. When any of these connect, it is important to redesign work to avoid overlaps or gaps that make the work inefficient or ineffective. New opportunities can also become apparent through system connections.

STh1: Reviewing of Operational Systems for Integration

Integrated thinking is not an immediate inclusion in everyday routines but it is the answer to many problems. Even though it is not an automatic instinct, it is worth trying to raise awareness of its value with operational system reviews for all to recognize how they work and impact each other. These workflow reviews raise the possibility of integrating work as it might benefit the organization and its knowledge workers.

STh2: Reviewing and Reflecting on Cases/Projects for Pivots

Review of projects and their outcomes, final and incremental, lends insight into needs for improvement in inputs and outcomes. The workflow and archetype analyses help with seeing obstacles and gaps that compromise outcomes. Structured discussions with team member contributors and external stakeholders will guide this review.

STh 3: Reflecting on and Maximizing Individual and Organizational Strengths

A leader identifies and maximizes individual and organizational strengths to develop and grow. When identified, both sets of strengths can find synergy to create new value for the organization, providing a great source of possibilities to grow. When people in an organization feel that they are appreciated for their contributions and expertise, they are more engaged and committed to the growth of the organization. This synergy between the individual and the organization can be uncovered to be a catalyst for new development and growth.

Reflection on strengths is the first step to establishing a practice that will create and sustain your company's growth culture. Discussions are most relevant when done in the context of a specific case study as they demonstrate real-time needs for these strengths.

An *Idea Box* should be available for any/all members to suggest a discussion topic or idea for improvement or new value. This box also should provide a standard protocol for structuring all entries.

STh4: Tracking Outcomes to Uncover New Opportunities, Guide Recognition and Rewards

Work is designed to create new value for an individual or an organization. A Benefits/Impact Summary is a record of the results of all work within an organization. This summary provides a way to track the benefits of your work and the impact that it creates. It is a focused way to ensure that all new value created is recognized. This recognition can also lead to a new project idea for further value creation to foster more individual or organizational development and growth. Chapter 8 "Reflections, New Value, and Celebrations" provides a sample Benefits/Impact Summary.

STh5: Reviewing Current Global, Regional, Industry, and Local Events and Trends to Uncover New Opportunities

The RFG team holds sessions to discuss the environment and its changing conditions, impact, events, and trends that might spark ideas for improvement and/or growth. All members are welcome and encouraged to attend. These discussions prompt members to examine their mindsets for alignment to external mindsets and uncovering new needs. These sessions are detailed in Chapter 8 "Reflections, New Value, and Celebrations."

Knowledge Work Templates

Often work can be structured using templates that prompt certain levels of inquiry, thinking, and research. Knowledge work is autonomous but can be facilitated with templates that guide the work. There are templates for building autonomous work components. Several are provided throughout this book as they pertain to related work practices. Others are available in an ancillary resource, "Developing the Intentional Mindset," which is available online through the publisher website.

Building an Autonomous Narrative for Your Organization

Narratives are discernable by industry, market, global expectations, professional standards, and employee perspectives. Different industries have different mindsets based on the nature of their work. Engineering companies will be very specific and exact in their mode of work. Retail stores will be very customer-conscious in their values, beliefs, behaviors, and decisions. Markets have the same diverse mindsets based on the customers who make up the market. Are customers focused on quality, or quantity, or on timeliness? Lawyers will value confidentiality and strict interpretation of the law. Additionally, some companies may be very employee focused as they see the employees as customers, first and foremost. When these mindsets are positively meaningful to stakeholders, they create a positive narrative for engagement and success.

These narratives are shaped by the mindset of the organization as leaders create it and behaviors are observed. They all have some version of the underlying characteristics listed earlier. Management theories and behaviors, motivators, satisfiers, and operational approaches are but a few ways that leaders create the narrative that others will follow. These elements of organizational mindset can be defined as an autonomous environment to host knowledge workers. They can also be more traditional in the environments that they create. In either case, the environment within the organization will set the work mode of its members and create the narrative of that organization to the world. This narrative can also encourage or discourage employee retention, satisfaction, and motivation.

When people have the data, tools, collaboration, and training needed to work autonomously, they feel that investment as a trusting, supportive, and achievement-oriented environment. It builds a sense of commitment and community. Enabling autonomous work with the resources available to answer queries or seek related research sends a message to all employees and stakeholders that learning is supported.

In today's 21st century knowledge economy, the autonomous environment serves organizations well in that it is attractive to the emerging workforce that has mastered remote working with knowledge work skills of autonomy. This environment translates for them into a sense of control of their own destinies and legacies.

Building an autonomous community can be done with mentoring, recognition, and rewards to support that narrative. Mode of work is a major indicator and example of an organization's values. How do actions, mentoring, recognition, and rewards reinforce activity to create community strengths and identity? What is obviously valued in your community? What is not reinforced? How does your organization confirm its narrative?

What actually is your organization's narrative? What are the tell-tale artifacts of your organization's narrative? How does this narrative align with your own narrative? How does your organization reinforce work in the context of this narrative? Does your organization use its narrative to attract and retain workers? The authenticity of a narrative and the mindset that drives it are often critical to individual and organizational success.

Awareness of what others think of you and your organization is important. A narrative is only relevant as others tell your story. What do others think of your organization? How does that narrative match your individual values? This would include an analysis of recent behaviors and decisions and their match to your stated values. If there is a gap, what behaviors might match your values better? How would you demonstrate that change to others so that your narrative is better defined by you as you desire it to be? You can be in control of your own narrative as an individual but only as a contributor to the narrative of your organization.

Leaders' Skills for Creating an Environment and Narrative

Organizations and their continuous change need strong leaders to navigate the changes with an environment that supports knowledge workers' autonomy (Shein 2021). The skills of these successful digital leaders include:

1. Adaptable: adapts to change and supports the transition from manual to digital processes, continuously communicates and facilitates as needs dictate
2. Capable of navigating uncertainty: lives with change and embraces ambiguity, promotes experimentation and agility, ensures a framework to manage risk
3. Adept at building relationships: measures success with adoption and uptake
4. Excellent communicators: communicates goals, tactics, and specific role contributions
5. Empathy: prioritizes that clients always come first, understands others' needs including workers
6. Capable of creating a culture of collaboration: empowers teams, encourages experimentation, incentivizes collaboration, and measures the performance of a team against business outcomes
7. Compelling storytelling: tells stories about the experience and achievements in the language of the listeners and not in the language of achievement, relates meaningfulness to those who need to understand

Reinforcing An Intended Narrative

Reinforcing your organizational narrative happens through the continuous reflection on outcomes, intended and actual. When there is a gap, there is a danger of rendering your narrative ineffective or, perhaps, even causing damage to your organization. Checking for gaps should provide insights into how and why the gap occurred and how to restore the organizational narrative to its intended state.

As noted for an individual's narrative, a gap may not be negative but just a mismatch of goals, values, or understanding of an issue. Uncovering and clarifying mismatches can lead to reconciliation of the gap and uphold your positive organizational narrative.

> **Can you think of a dimension of your organization that does not match its intended narrative?**

Organizational Structures and Narrative

Organizations have narratives that tell their stories. If an organization is autonomous, it will have that narrative. Is it a good place to work? Do leaders support your ideas? What is the culture like? Do people work together well?

Leaders of 21st century organizations can ensure an autonomous environment and narrative by building the following characteristics into their organizations:

- Organizational mindset and narrative are defined and shared, including performance and learning goals and mode of work.
- Mindset awareness and alignment are required and supported with relevant data and information for individuals, stakeholders, organizations, and partners.
- Digital nervous system is available and used for data and information support and analysis of economic feasibility, mindset, future state, workflow and archetype analysis, decision influencers, and choice architectures.
- Confidence, inquiry, and learning-orientation are built and supported through the learning system structure, prior learning references, teams and projects, personal profiles, autonomous decision making, economic and mindset evaluation, archetype workflow analysis, and future state speculation.
- Recognition and reward for new value creators/contributors and awareness of percent of contribution are integral parts of the organization.
- Growth and reflection team sessions are regularly held to uncover, support, and reinforce new ideas.
- An intentional balance of management theories, satisfiers, and motivators is prevalent.

What organizational narrative is attractive to you? As a member? As a leader?

How does a leader create this environment to support autonomous work in your organization?

Worksheet Reference

Worksheets to facilitate using the concepts in this chapter are found in "Developing the Intentional Mindset, Module 7: Building an Autonomous Environment." The worksheets include:

Individual Autonomy
Organizational Environment for Autonomy

Call to Action

Set up individual productivity and organizational performance metrics and measures to align with goals.

1. Check the overarching workflow of your organization to find obstacles to meeting those metrics and measures.
2. What mindset component has created these obstacles?
3. Does your workflow demonstrate an autonomous environment?
4. Do your productivity and performance metrics demonstrate this environment?
5. Reflect on your organization to diagnose the factors that could make it exceptionally autonomous for the best use of all efforts.
6. Make a plan to implement those factors.

Chapter Summary

This chapter describes the environment that leaders will want to create to prompt 21st century autonomous work for best growth results for individuals and for the organization as a whole.

Glossary

These terms are uniquely defined in the context of developing an intentional mindset

Artifact: A tangible sign of a goal, a value, a belief, or mode of work

Attributes: Descriptors of an individual, a group, an organization, or an artifact

Autonomy: The ability to be in control, to be independent, and to recognize dependence for complementary skills or knowledge

Awareness: Continuous observation and acknowledgment of relevant factors or occurrences

Behavioral economists: Economists who study the source and impact of decision behaviors on economic factors

Behavioral tendencies: The behaviors that describe an individual or group's tendencies or rationale for decision making

Behaviors: Individual and group actions

Beliefs: Opinions, assumptions, and biases regarding a specific subject, individual, or group

Beliefs and mode of work alignment: Beliefs that drive various modes of work

Benefits/Impact Summary: Summary chart for tracking progress as it impacts an individual or an organization

Biases, implicit and explicit: Implicit beliefs that are unconscious; explicit beliefs that are conscious and intentional

Bloom's taxonomy of seven levels of thinking: Incrementally defined thinking for expanding awareness and understanding of the factors leading to value creation, including remembering, understanding, applying, analyzing, synthesizing, evaluating, and creating

Brainsteering: Limited considerations of a specific domain for ideation

Brainstorming: Unlimited considerations of all domains for ideation

Celebration: Congratulatory practices, recognition, or reward for new value creation

Choice architectures: Decision choices that facilitate an individual's ability to decide

Co-intrapreneuring: Multiple individuals working together within an organization to find efficiencies or new value

Collaboration: Individuals or groups working together toward a common goal

Communications personas/styles—politician, preacher, prosecutor, scientist: Various approaches to communicating with others

Communications plan: Audience-specific focus for all messaging

Communications stages—Readiness, Relevance, Reinforcement, Reflection: Stages of incremental communication that facilitate collaborators' understanding and engagement

Community mentality: Common goals, values, beliefs, and modes of work of a group that incents like behaviors from members of the group

Compassion: Understanding, relating, and sympathy for another's misfortune or condition from one's own experiences

Confirmation: The need to validate an individual's current belief

Connecting goals and values: The agreement of goals and values to support resulting behaviors

Conservative: A sense of individual self-sufficiency and responsibility, free markets, and privatization

Consumption chain: An individual's or an organization's connections to all areas of consuming

Contextual links: An individual's or organization's background factors that provide understanding of behaviors and decisions

Conversation starters: Facilitators for engaging in conversations that build trust and relationships

Culture: The mindset and environment within which one lives

Data: Objectively-collected facts and statistics that lend themselves to interpretation, analysis, and evaluation

Data analysis: Descriptive, exploratory, inferential, predictive, causal, mechanistic, and regressive for responding to related inquiry

Data collection: Collecting data and information that is relevant to an issue or inquiry, such as brainstorming or brainsteering

Decision influencers: Data and/or information that sheds new light on a decision point

Decision making: Actions and behaviors that lead to a result

Decision rationale: Background/mindset thinking that drives a decision

Desired outcomes: The intended and optimal, per individual perspective/mindset, results of actions and behaviors

Destiny: One's personal vision for life achievement

Digital nervous system: System that provides data and information to support relevant data analysis

Economic analysis: Inquiry into economic factors of supply and demand, opportunity costs, production possibilities, and externalities to quantify options

Emotional analysis: Inquiry into mindset of all stakeholders as it relates to the mindset of a project

Entitlement: Belief that an individual or organization is owed something without earning it

Entrepreneuring: The pursuit of ideation and new value within a global and external context

Experiences: All life's events and activities that create a frame for mindset development

Five Whys: Sequential analysis of events, trends, activities, or decisions that create understanding of causal, correlating, and contributing factors to a situation

Flow of thinking: Extremely consuming and effective state of thinking that enables complete focus on one's work

Giver, taker, matcher: Descriptions of behaviors and outcomes of individuals who consistently and continuously give, take, or match contributions when working with others

Global value dimensions: A set of values that are consistently held throughout the world to varying degrees within each nation

Goal categories: Goals in personal, professional, community, and expertise domains

Goals: Aspirations for achievement in support of one's vision and the pursuits to support that vision

Growth: Measured progress toward a goal

Heuristics: Activity that follows previous rationale without consideration of new circumstances

Hierarchy of goals: Incremental sequence of goals that support and lead to mastery of an ultimate goal

Idea Box: Freely accessible repository for anyone's idea that has been quantified and qualified according to preliminary and defined protocols

Independent, dependent, interdependent: Modes of work that integrate to support autonomous activity and environment

Information: Meaning extracted by analysis and application of data collected and referenced

Inquiry: A continuous interest and questioning of surrounding activity, decisions, and causes

Integration of operations: Awareness and understanding of how operational input and outcome impact each other

Intrapreneuring: The pursuit of ideation and new value within an organization

Invisible capital: One's connections, experiences, and subsequent knowledge that enhances one's skills, capabilities, and resources

Journaling: The practice of recording and reflecting on current occurrences for later considerations

Knowledge: Situational meaning extracted from data and information when analyzed, synthesized, and evaluated for new meaning and value creation

Knowledge economy: The economic state in which knowledge as a resource is most important as it guides the use of other resources of land, labor, and capital

Learning: Structured inquiry, research, analysis, and conclusion for new value creation

Learning context: The situation to be evaluated and the background mindsets that will shape activity and decisions

Learning and performance: Learning activities that support achieving a goal, which is performance-based

Learning mindset: One's goals, values, beliefs, and modes of work that are aligned with continuous, consistent, and comprehensive learning

Learning modes: Eight learning styles, including linguistic, logical/mathematical, spatial, bodily kinesthetic, musical, interpersonal, intrapersonal, and naturalist

Learning system: Six steps that ensure learning, including mindset awareness, entrepreneurial options, economic quantification, emotional/mindset qualification, project implementation, and reflection

Legacy: One's professional goals for achievement

Levels of influence: Stakeholders with differing levels of interest, influence, and impact on one's work, prioritizing levels of attention needed

Liberal: Free spirited, wide views, supportive of individual rights

Listening: A focus on a message in its completeness, including words, tone, body language, and rationale

Management theories X, Y, Z: Theories that guide management of employees for optimal productivity and performance, giving various levels and types of guidance for completing assigned work

Maslow's five levels of needs and development: Physiological, security, belonging, esteem, and self-actualization to be achieved in sequence

Matching mindset components: Aligning mindset components of goals, values, beliefs, and modes of work to ensure complementary and non conflicting work activities or decisions

Measures: Tools used to track progress toward a metric goal

Metrics: The relevant measurement to define a desired outcome of goal achievement

Mindful presence: Awareness of one's own and others' mindsets and needs

Mind mapping: Systematic practice of joining and aligning considerations and options identified during brainstorming and brainsteering activities

Mindset: What one thinks, how one thinks, why one thinks what one thinks as manifested in one's goals, values, beliefs, and mode of work, leads to one's narrative

Mindset components: Goals, values, beliefs, and mode of work

Mindset source: Elements of life that have formed one's mindset, including nature and nurture, strengths, experiences, community mentality, and uncertainties of life

Mission: The pursuit of projects, work, and goals that support the pursuit of one's vision

Mode of work: The practices and protocols that guide one's work individually and with others, should be influenced by goals, values, and beliefs

Narrative: The story of oneself, held by oneself and by others

Narrative, intended versus actual: Intended narrative desired, actual narrative of others' perspectives

Nature: The mindset cause that is derived by birth

Neural mirrors: The response messaging that communicates what the messenger conveyed, seen in facial expressions

Nurture: The mindset cause that is derived from the upbringing one receives

Observing others: A vehicle for understanding others and for insights into one's own activities, behaviors, decisions, their causes, and the perceptions of others

Opinions and assumptions: One's biases based on mindset causes, not factual but subjective in nature

Organizational profile: Description of an organization's mindset, including goals, values, beliefs, and mode of work as context that sets the environment for knowledge workers

Original research: Surveys, conversations, interviews, and so on that are designed to collect very specific and genuine data and information regarding a scenario or stakeholder mindset and needs

Performance: The achievement of an individual or organizational goal, incremental or ultimate

Persistence: The ability to persevere through obstacles, gaps, lack of support to continue efforts toward an ultimate goal

Potential for success: Belief that the capacity for achieving success is universal

Predictive: Foreseeing and forecasting future conditions, events, trends, and decisions

Prescriptive: Directing activity toward a goal

Prioritizing stakeholders: Investing in engagement based on the level of influence (see previous definition)

Productivity: Level of individual achievement toward an individual goal

Profiling: Describing the complete mindset of someone, including sources of mindset components

Progress tracking: Recording work and value created by that work

Projects: Structured and sequential work that includes mindset considerations

Protocols: Behavioral expectations on how work will be done within an organization or an individual's perspectives

Queries: Relevant inquiry into how, what, when, where, and who about a situation, obstacle, issue, or unexpected success

Recognition: Calling attention to a desired activity, behavior, or decision to reinforce its continuance

Reflection: In hindsight reviewing activities, behaviors, and outcomes for new learning

Rethinking: Awareness of the need to pause for reconsideration of a heuristic response to a situation or need

Rewards: Giving a tangible and earned gift to reward a desired activity, behavior, or decision to reinforce its continuance

Satisfaction and motivation: Satisfaction is a minimal requirement for employment retention, motivation instigates forward thinking, growth, and new value creation

Self-sufficiency: The ability to take control of one's self to direct activities, behaviors, and decisions in one's best interest as aligned with goals and values

Seven frames of opportunity by Drucker: Seven opportunities to consider when intrapreneuring or entrepreneuring, including unexpected success and failures, incongruities, process need, industry and market structures, demographics, changes in perception, and new knowledge

Shareholders: The financial owners of a venture, initiative, or effort

Stakeholders: All who impact one's work in any way or degree of influence

Stakeholder communications by Jensen: Communicating with consideration of audience, their needs, one's desired actions, and most feasible formatting of the message

Stakeholders' profiles: Descriptions of stakeholders, their mindsets, mindset sources, and needs

Status quo: The application of heuristics in decision making

Strengths: What one is very good at naturally, an intuitive ability

System One, reactionary response: Actions, behaviors, and decisions that are immediate and do not consider options, usually based on a heuristic approach

System Two, consideration and reaction: Actions, behaviors, and decisions that are not spontaneous, allowing time for consideration and evaluation of relevant queries and factors that impact the response

Trends and events: Global, national, regional, and local externalities that need monitoring and awareness for potential options and opportunities for growth

Trust building: An intentional endeavor for building stakeholdership

Uncertainties: All unpredictable, unprecedented, and shocking conditions that impact one's life and sustainability

Values: The core principles by which one lives one's life

Values and goals alignment: Values and goals are complementary, support each other, and are usually thought of together; see "connecting goals and values," defined earlier

Vision: The destiny and legacy plans that one creates for oneself

Workflow/archetype analysis: Study of actual inputs, outcomes, and expectations to uncover obstacles, gaps, and opportunities for greater effectiveness and/or efficiencies

References

Ackoff, R.L., J. Magidson, and H.J. Addison. 2006. *Idealized Design Creating an Organization's Future.* Upper Saddle River, NJ: Wharton School Publishing.

Akerlof, G. and R. Kranston. 2011. *Identity Economics.* Princeton, NJ: Princeton University Press.

Ariely, D. 2009. *Predictably Irrational.* New York, NY: HarperCollins Publishers.

Ariely, D. 2010. *The Upside of Irrationality: The Unexpected Benefits of Defying Logic.* New York, NY: Harper Perennial.

Armstrong, P. 2010. *Bloom's Taxonomy.* Nashville, TN: Vanderbilt University Center for Teaching.

Asplund, J. and B.J. Brim. 2023. *The Powerful Duo of Strengths and Engagement.* Washington, DC: Gallup, Inc.

Association of American Colleges and Universities. 2009. *A Global Learning Value Rubric.* Washington, DC.

Baird, D. 2022. Interview by J. Frankel.

Bodhipaksa. 2014. "We Are What We Think." Tricycle. www.tricycle.org.

Brooks, D. 2012. *The Social Animal.* New York, NY: Random House Trade Paperbacks.

Brooks, D. 2016. *The Road to Character.* New York, NY: Random House Trade Paperbacks.

Brooks, D. 2020. "Conversation Starters Nine Non-obvious Ways to Have Deeper Conversations." *New York Times.*

Brooks, D. 2021. "Is Self-Awareness a Mirage?" *New York Times.*

Brooks, D. 2022. "What the Beatles Tell Us About Fame." *New York Times.*

Brown, D. and R.K. Crace, 1996. "Life Values Inventory." Life Values Resources. pinnowedna@charter.net.

Chalofsky, N. 2003. "Meaningful Work." *Training and Development.*

Chernow, R. 2004. *Alexander Hamilton.* New York, NY: Penguin Group (USA) Inc.

Covey, S. 1989. *The Seven Habits of Highly Effective People.* New York, NY: Simon and Schuster.

Coyle, D. 2013. "What's your LQ (Learning Quotient)?" danielcoyle.com.

Csikszentmihalyi, M. 2008. *Flow.* New York, NY: HarperCollins Publishers.

Davenport, T. and J. Kim. 2018. *HBR Guide to Data Analytics Basics for Managers.* Boston: Harvard Business Review Press.

Denworth, L. 2020. "Conservative and Liberal Brains Might Have Some Real Differences." *Scientific American.*

Drucker, P. 1985. *Innovation and Entrepreneurship*. New York, NY: HarperCollins Publishers, Inc.

Drucker, P. 1994. *Post-Capitalist Society*. New York, NY: Harper Business Publisher, A Division of HarperCollins Publishers.

Drucker, P. 1999. "Managing Oneself." *Harvard Business Review*.

Duckworth, A. 2018. *Grit The Power of Passion and Perseverance*. New York, NY: Scribner, An Imprint of Simon and Schuster, Inc.

Dweck, C.S. 2016. *Mindset*. New York, NY: Balantine Books, An Imprint and Division of Penguin Random House LLC.

Frank, R.H. 2016. *Success and Luck Good Fortune and the Myth of Meritocracy*. Princeton and Oxford: Princeton University Press.

Friedman, T. 2016. *Thank You for Being Late*. New York, NY: Farrar, Straus and Giroux.

Fuhrmans, V. and L. Weber. 2021. "Redefining Ambition." *Wall Street Journal*.

Galef, J. 2021. *The Scout Mindset Why Some People See Things Clearly and Others Don't*. New York, NY: Portfolio/Penguin.

Gardner, H. 1993. *Multiple Intelligences*. New York, NY: BasicBooks, A Subsidiary of Perseus Books, LLC

Gardner, H. 1995. *Leading Minds*. New York, NY: BasicBooks, A Division of HarperCollins Publishers, Inc.

Gates, B. 1999. *Business@The Speed of Thought*. New York, NY: Warner Books, Inc.

Gill, A. 2021. "Economists Explain the Taliban." *The Wall Street Journal*.

Goleman, D. 2005. *Emotional Intelligence*. New York, NY: Bantam Dell, A Division of Random House, Inc.

Goleman, D. 2006. *Social Intelligence*. New York, NY: Bantam Dell, A Division of Random House, Inc.

Goodwin, D.K. 1994. *No Ordinary Times*. New York, NY: Simon and Schuster Paperbacks.

Goodwin, D.K. 2006. *A Team of Rivals*. New York, NY: Simon and Schuster Paperbacks.

Grant, A. 2014. *Give and Take Why Helping Others Gives Us Success*. New York, NY: Penguin Books.

Grant, A. 2021. *Think Again*. New York, NY: VIKING, An imprint of Penguin Random House LLC.

Haidt, J. 2012. *The Righteous Mind*. New York, NY: Pantheon books, a Division of Random House, Inc.

Hofstede, G., G.J. Hofstede, and M. Minkov. 2010. *Cultures and Organizations Software of the Mind*. New York, NY: McGraw Hill.

Howell, G. 2006. *Gertrude Bell Queen of the Desert, Shaper of Nations*. New York, NY: Farrar, Straus and Giroux.

Huber, C. and K. Sneader. 2021. "The Eight Trends That Will Define 2021 and Beyond." *McKinsey and Company Podcast.*

Jensen, B. 2000. *Simplicity, The New Competitive Advantage.* New York, NY: Perseus Books.

Johnson, B.C., J.M. Manyika, and L.A. Yee. 2005. "The Next Revolution in Interactions." *McKinsey Quarterly.*

Kahneman, D. 2011. *Thinking, Fast and Slow.* New York, NY: Farrar, Straus and Giroux.

Kang, C. and R. Mac. 2021. "Whistle-Blower Says Facebook 'Chooses Profits Over Safety'." *New York Times.*

Kennedy, A. and T. Deal. 2000. *Corporate Cultures.* New York, NY: BasicBooks, a member of Perseus Books Publishing, LLC.

Kepner, T. 2021. "Don Sutton Had an 'Easy Job' Thanks to a Lifetime of Hard Work." *New York Times.*

Kleiner, A., C. Roberts, R.B. Ross, P.M. Senge, and B.J. Smith, 1994. *The Fifth Discipline Fieldbook.* New York, NY: Doubleday A Division of Bantam Doubleday Dell Publishing Group.

Lomangino, K.M. 2015. "Countering Cognitive Bias: Tips for Recognizing the Impact of Potential Bias on Research." *Journal of the Academy of Nutrition and Dietetics.*

MacGregor, D. 2006. *The Human Side of Enterprise.* New York, NY: McGraw-Hill Companies.

McGrath, R. and I. MacMillan. 2000. *The Entrepreneurial Mindset.* Boston, Mass: Harvard Business School Press.

Meyer, M.C. 1978. "Six Stages of Demotivation." *IEEE Engineering Management Review.*

Mitra, R. 2017. "Tell Me a Story: Narratives, Behaviour Change and Neuroscience." *BBC Blogs.*

Moore, W. 2011. *The Other Wes Moore.* New York, NY: Spiegel & Grau Trade Paperbacks.

Nickerson, C. 2023. "Herzberg's Motivation Two-Factor Theory." *London, England:* Simply Psychology for Simply Scholar Ltd.

Ouchi, W. 1981. *Theory Z: How American Business Can Meet the Japanese Challenge.* Reading, Mass: Addison-Wesley Publishing Company, Inc.

Perel, E. 2021. "Uncertainty Doesn't Have to Mean Anxiety." *The Wall Street Journal.*

Posth, M. 2008. *1,000 Days in Shanghai.* Singapore: John Wiley & Sons (Asia).

Raab, C. 2010. *Invisible Capital.* Oakland, CA: Berrett-Kohler Publishers.

Rapaille, C. 2006. *The Culture Code.* New York, NY: Broadway Books.

Rolnik, G. and R. Shapira. 2020. "President-Elect Joe Biden and the Real Lessons of DuPont." *Oxford Business Law Blog.*

Sachs, H. 2022. *What Is Theory X and Theory Y, What Is the Practical Application of Theory Y Approach to Management, The Benefits of Managers Using the Theory Y Management Style to Manage Employees, and the Problems With Managers Using the Theory X Management Style.* Middletown, Delaware.

Safronova, V. 2021, "How Women Are Changing the Philanthropy Game." *New York Times.*

Salisbury, S. 2020. "Artful Medicine." *The Philadelphia Inquirer.*

Schawbel, D. 2018. "Fighting the Loneliness Epidemic at Work." *Rescue Time Blog.*

Schumpeter, J. 1934. *The Theory of Economic Development.* Boston, Mass: Harvard University Press.

Serrat, S. 2009. *The Five Whys Technique.* Manila, Philippines: Asian Development Bank.

Shealy, C.N. 2016. *Making Sense of Beliefs and Values: Theory, Research, and Practice.* New York, NY: Springer Publishing.

Shein, E. 2021. "7 Skills of Successful Digital Leaders." *CIO Magazine.*

Shiller, R. 2019. *Narrative Economics.* Princeton, NJ: Princeton University Press.

Smith, L. 2017. *Meet Maslow.* Middletown, Delaware: Make Profits Easy LLC.

St. Joseph Montessori School. 2023. *Website Mission Statement.*

Starke, R. 2013. "Defining a Vision: Making Sure Your Work Matters." *Brand Identity, Creativity, Web Strategy.*

Starke, R. 2022. Interview by J. Frankel.

Taylor, A. 2021. "So Many Stakeholders. How Do Companies Choose Who to Satisfy?" *Wall Street Journal.*

Thaler, R. and C. Sunstein. 2008. *Nudge.* New York, NY: Penguin Books.

Thaler, R. 2016. *Misbehaving: The Making of Behavioral Economics.* New York, NY: W.W. Norton & Company.

Upwork Study. 2020. *Press Release: Upwork Study Finds 22% of American Workforce Will Be Remote by 2025.* www.upwork.com/press/releases/upwork-study-finds-22-of-american-workforce-will-be-remote-by-2025.

Vedantam, S. and B. Mesler. 2021 *Useful Delusions the Power and Paradox of the Self-Deceiving Brain.* New York, NY: S. S. Norton & Company, Inc.

Waitzkin, J. 2007. *The Art of Learning.* New York, NY: Free Press, A Division of Simon and Schuster, Inc.

Weiner, J. 2018. "How Compassion Builds Better Companies." *Linkedin: Graduation speech.*

World Values Research, 1981. "World Values Survey." Vienna, Austria: World Values Association.

Wunderer, R. 2001. "Employees as Co-intrapreneuring, A Transformation Concept." *Leadership and Organization Development Journal.*

Zynga, A. 2014. *A Social Brain is a Smarter Brain.* Brighton, Mass: Harvard Business Review.

About the Author

Jane Frankel is the Managing Principal of The Art of Performance LLC, which she founded in 2007. Frankel has been an advocate of lifelong learning throughout her career as a teacher, organizational design specialist, and program developer in both the private and public sectors. Her focus is on building 21st century innovation and learning cultures through workforce and customer engagement, strategic alliances, internships, and innovation planning. Frankel has developed multiple innovation programs requiring the collaboration of diverse mindsets. These programs include:

- Customized curriculum to serve diverse student needs and capabilities
- Customer service alignment to customer needs and mindsets
- Strategic partnerships with external experts for new product and services development and delivery
- Mentor structures for project design and implementation
- Project-based internships between the emerging workforce and external employers for job placement
- Knowledge Work Institute (LinkedIn platform) to socialize the needs and uses of knowledge and its impact for social media audience

Frankel holds an MS degree in Organizational Dynamics from the University of PA and an MS in Education from Temple University, both in Philadelphia, PA. Previously, Frankel was an advisory board member for the Center for Regional Economics at Temple University, Society for Technical Communication, Association for Talent Development, a former member of the Middle Market Steering Committee for the Greater Philadelphia Chamber of Commerce, has served as the Cochair of the Programming Committee for the Entrepreneurs' Forum of Greater Philadelphia, a board member of BEACON (formerly GPSEG)

Executive Networking Group, Chair of the GPSEG Mentoring Committee, and a member of the Network for Women in Computers and Technology (NWCT). She has published *Expert Perspectives* on the National Center for Middle Market website and for her *Knowledge Work Institute* on LinkedIn.

Index

Concise and Applied Business Books

The Collection listed above is one of 30 business subject collections that Business Expert Press has grown to make BEP a premiere publisher of print and digital books. Our concise and applied books are for...

- Professionals and Practitioners
- Faculty who adopt our books for courses
- Librarians who know that BEP's Digital Libraries are a unique way to offer students ebooks to download, not restricted with any digital rights management
- Executive Training Course Leaders
- Business Seminar Organizers

Business Expert Press books are for anyone who needs to dig deeper on business ideas, goals, and solutions to everyday problems. Whether one print book, one ebook, or buying a digital library of 110 ebooks, we remain the affordable and smart way to be business smart. For more information, please visit www.businessexpertpress.com, or contact sales@businessexpertpress.com.

www.ingramcontent.com/pod-product-compliance
Lightning Source LLC
Chambersburg PA
CBHW061149220326
41599CB00025B/4419